Frances Dyer

New world pilgrims at old world shrines

The book of the pilgrimage

Frances Dyer

New world pilgrims at old world shrines
The book of the pilgrimage

ISBN/EAN: 9783337291136

Printed in Europe, USA, Canada, Australia, Japan

Cover: Foto ©Lupo / pixelio.de

More available books at **www.hansebooks.com**

A. E. Dunning   Harriet W. Dunning,
                Jamaica Plain.

Morton Dexter
    Boston —   Emily Buehner and Dunning
                Jamaica Plain,

Wm. L. Whittemore
    Boston USA   Charles H. Noyes.
                 Nashua, N. H.

Chas. Liffler Jr.
    Boston   Cyrus Richardson

F. D. Sargent   Edwin Knight Holden
                 Bridgeport Ct.

Lucinda E. Peobie   Edward Rohr
   Greenland   Greenland, N. H.
      N. H.
                 Mary E. Pierce
                    Whitman Massachusetts
Frances J. Dyer
   Boston — Mass. William E. Park
                    Gloversville, N.Y.
Anna F. Burnham
  Cambridge, Mass. Alonzo S. Wallace

Matthew A. Laue
Boston

Fannie Foster Brown
Hartford
Conn.

Onslow C. Stanett
Sheldon
Iowa

Stephen Scott
Jamaica Plain

Ellen In Case
Hartford
Conn.

Carrie A. Hyde
San Francisco
Calif.

Minnie U. Scott
Magazine
Arkansas

Wm. W. Leete
Rockford Illinois

Emily P Rand
Taunton
Mass.

Marion Rice Prouty
Spencer
Mass.

Mrs Charles N Prouty
Spencer
Massachusetts

Wilbur Wheeler

R. P. Hibbard
Gloucester, Mass.

Caroline M. Galpin
New Haven
Conn.

Sherrod Soule
Naugatuck
Conn.

Harriet Powell
Hartford
Conn.

Mary R. Storrs
Brooklyn
N. Y.

Nathan W. Littlefield
Pawtucket
R. I.

Mary W. Littlefield
Pawtucket
R. I.

Alice G. West
Trinity, R. I.

Laura E. Seymour
Bristol
Conn.

Rebecca Thacher Liffler
Boston
Mass.

Ellen M. Pomeroy
Reading
Penn.

Wm. A. Robinson.
Middletown.
N. Y.

Lucy S. Robinson.
Middletown
New York.

Mrs. A. L. Goodrich
Hartford
Conn.

Mary J. McAdoo.
North Bloomfield
Ohio.

George T. Ewink
San Francisco
California

Lucy A. Brainard.
Hartford, Conn.

Ahr. Mackennal
Bowdon, Ches.

George Hardy
London

Effie Mackennal

W. B. Wright
London

Edwin Joshua Dukes
Bridgwater, England

The Book of The Pilgrimage

THE CONGREGATIONALIST'S PILGRIMAGE to England and Holland was first announced in the Souvenir Membership List of the Oriental Tour organized by us in the spring of 1895. These two important schemes of travel signalize the one the opening and the other the completion of the 80th year of the life of the paper. The Oriental Tour brought together a large company of ladies and gentlemen of congenial tastes, and a very extended journey through Eastern lands was successfully accomplished without mishap. The Pilgrimage naturally included a still larger membership, and proved to be of even greater interest. The National Council of Congregational Churches of the United States recognized its representative character by appointing a special committee to represent the Council in connection with the tour, and a distinguished coöperating committee was organized in England. It may therefore be properly claimed that the enterprise was of international significance, and its success was due on the one hand to the prompt response and widespread interest which the plan of The Pilgrimage awakened in the United States, and on the other, to the cordial and hospitable attitude of our English friends towards the visit of these New-World Pilgrims to Old-World Shrines.

※ ※ ※

THE PILGRIMAGE LETTERS which appeared weekly in the columns of The Congregationalist were written by Miss Frances J. Dyer, one of the editors of the paper, who was a member of the party. So admirably and so faithfully did these letters chronicle the experiences of the journey that they have been made the basis of The Book of The Pilgrimage. Much material has been added, but the original letter form has been retained in order that the personal and familiar touch of the first account may not be lost.

※ ※ ※

THE ILLUSTRATIONS in The Book of The Pilgrimage have been gathered from many sources. Rev. William White Leete, one of the pilgrims, was very successful with his camera, and we are indebted to him for several unique views. Most of the pictures of Pilgrim localities, both in England and Holland, are from photographs specially taken for us by the well-known artist, Clifton Johnson. The frontispiece, title-page, and finis, and all the initial letters have been drawn by L. S. Ipsen. The significant initial designs will repay study, and are briefly described on page 10. We are glad to recognize here our indebtedness to many English firms, whose photographs we have reproduced in the following pages.

W. L. GREENE & COMPANY.

Office of THE CONGREGATIONALIST,
Congregational House, Boston, Mass., U. S. A.
1st December, 1899.

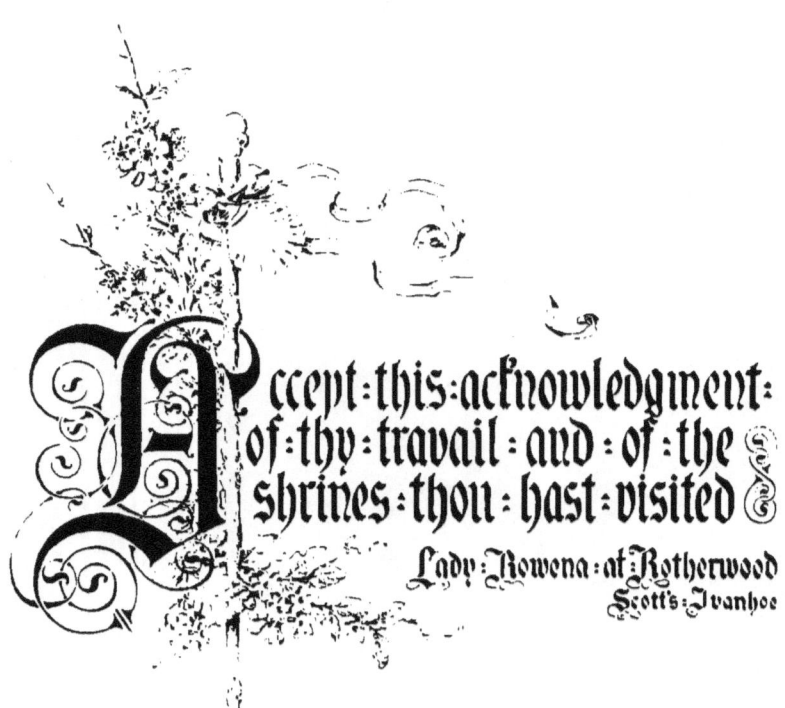

Accept this acknowledgment of thy travail and of the shrines thou hast visited

Lady Rowena at Rotherwood
Scott's Ivanhoe

New World Pilgrims at old World Shrines

The Book of The Pilgrimage

A · RECORD OF · THE · CONGREGATIONALIST'S · PILGRIMAGE TO · ENGLAND · AND · HOLLAND · MDCCCXCVI · PUBLISHED · AT · THE · OFFICE · OF · THE · CONGREGATIONALIST · CONGREGATIONAL · HOUSE · BOSTON · MASSACHUSETTS · U. · S. · A.

THE CONGREGATIONALIST, W. L. GREENE & COMPANY, PROPRIETORS, BOSTON, MASSACHUSETTS, U. S. A.

COPYRIGHT BY W. L. GREENE & COMPANY, 1896

To our Hosts in England

especially to those whose names are inscribed below, this Book of The Pilgrimage, which records very inadequately their gracious hospitality, is respectfully

DEDICATED

THE MOST REV. WILLIAM ALEXANDER, D.D., D.C.L., Lord Archbishop of Armagh, Primate of All Ireland.
THE RIGHT HON. THE EARL OF ANCASTER, P.C., Joint Hereditary Lord Great Chamberlain of England.
REV. CHARLES ISAAC ATHERTON, M.A., Treasurer and Canon Residentiary of Exeter Cathedral.
REV. DAVID BARNETT, Congregational Minister, Boston.
REV. GEORGE SLATTYER BARRETT, B.A., D.D., Norwich (Member of The Pilgrimage Reception Committee).
WILSON BARRETT, ESQ., London.
REV. CHARLES ALBERT BERRY, D.D., Wolverhampton, Chairman (1897) of the Congregational Union of England and Wales (Member of The Pilgrimage Reception Committee).
GENERAL SIR MICHAEL ANTHONY SHRAPNEL BIDDULPH, G.C.B., the Gentleman Usher of the Black Rod.
REV. W. BLACKSHAW, B.A., B.D., Congregational Minister, Boston.
J. T. BOND, ESQ., The Right Worshipful the Mayor of Plymouth.
MRS. BOND.
REV. GEORGE HUGH BOURNE, D.C.L., Sub-Dean of Salisbury.
VERY REV. GEORGE DAVID BOYLE, M.A., Dean of Salisbury.
VERY REV. GEORGE GRANVILLE BRADLEY, D.D., Dean of Westminster, Dean of The Most Honourable Order of the Bath, Chaplain-in-Ordinary to the Queen.
REV. JOHN BROWN, D.D., Bedford, Chairman of Congregational Union Committee (Member of The Pilgrimage Reception Committee).
REV. HENRY MONTAGU BUTLER, D.D., Master of Trinity College, Cambridge; Chaplain-in-Ordinary to the Queen.
J. CLARKE, ESQ., The Right Worshipful the Mayor of Boston.
REV. JACOB CLEMENTS, M.A., Sub-Dean and Canon Residentiary of Lincoln.
J. J. COLMAN, ESQ., J.P., Norwich.
A. W. W. DALE, ESQ., M.A., Tutor in Trinity Hall, Cambridge.
THE RIGHT REV. RANDALL THOMAS DAVIDSON, D.D., Lord Bishop of Winchester, Prelate of the Order of the Garter.
MRS. DAVIDSON.
REV. C. E. DICKINSON, Congregational Minister, Winchester.
ARTHUR RAYNER DYER, ESQ., the Right Worshipful the Mayor of Winchester.
REV. WALTER JOHN EDMONDS, B.D., Canon of Exeter Cathedral.
REV. W. JUSTIN EVANS, Congregational Minister, Exeter (now of Lewisham, London).
REV. ANDREW M. FAIRBAIRN, D.D., LL.D., Principal of Mansfield College, Oxford.
VERY REV. FREDERIC WILLIAM FARRAR, D.D., Dean of Canterbury.
REV. P. T. FORSYTH, D.D., Congregational Minister, Cambridge.
REV. HUGH S. GRIFFITHS, Pastor of John Robinson Memorial Church, Gainsborough.
THE RIGHT HON. WILLIAM COURT GULLY, Speaker of the House of Commons.
REV. NEWMAN HALL, D.D., LL.B., London.
EDWARD HARRISON, ESQ., The Right Worshipful the Mayor of Lincoln.
REV. WILLIAM HARDY HARWOOD, Minister of Union Chapel, Islington, London.
REV. EDWARD HASSAN, Congregational Minister, Salisbury.
REV. WALTER P. HOGBEN, Congregational Minister, Glastonbury.

To our Hosts in England

REV. R. F. HORTON, M.A., D.D. (Member of The Pilgrimage Reception Committee).
REV. JOHN DANIEL JONES, M.A., B.D., Congregational Minister, Lincoln.
THE RIGHT REV. GEORGE WYNDHAM KENNION, D.D., the Lord Bishop of Bath and Wells.
REV. T. J. KIGHTLEY, Congregational Minister, Wells.
VERY REV. WILLIAM LEFROY, D.D., Dean of Norwich.
REV. JOHN LEWIS, Congregational Minister, Norwich.
MRS. G. S. LISTER, Finningley Park, Austerfield.
REV. ALEXANDER MACKENNAL, B.A., D.D., Bowdon (Chairman of The Pilgrimage Reception Committee).
REV. J. TOWNSEND MAXWELL, Congregational Minister, Plymouth.
REV. ANDREW MEARNS, Secretary of London Congregational Union (Member of The Pilgrimage Reception Committee).
REV. FREDERICK BROTHERTON MEYER, B.A., Minister of Christ Church, Westminster-bridge-road, London.
E. MINSHALL, ESQ., Editor of The Nonconformist Musical Journal, London.
REV. WILLIAM MOTTRAM, Traveling Secretary of Congregational Total Abstinence Association, London.
D. MUNSEY, ESQ., Cambridge.
MRS. MUNSEY.
REV. JOSEPH PARKER, D.D., Minister of The City Temple, London.
EDWARD F. PYE-SMITH, ESQ., J.P., Ex-Mayor of Salisbury.
REV. JAMES GUINNESS ROGERS, D.D., Clapham (Member of The Pilgrimage Reception Committee).
THE RIGHT REV. JOHN SHEEPSHANKS, D.D., Lord Bishop of Norwich.
VENERABLE WILLIAM MACDONALD SINCLAIR, D.D., Archdeacon of London, and Canon Residentiary of St. Paul's Cathedral.
NORMAN H. SMITH, ESQ., M.A., Secretary, Mansfield College, Oxford.
THE LADY HENRY SOMERSET, Reigate Priory, Surrey.
VERY REV. W. R. WOOD STEPHENS, B.D., Dean of Winchester.
REV. JOHN STEPHENSON, M.A., Vicar of Boston.
REV. WILLIAM ERNEST STEPHENSON, Congregational Minister, Canterbury.
HALLEY STEWART, ESQ., J.P., The Firs, Clapham Park, London.
MRS. STEWART.
VERY REV. CHARLES W. STUBBS, M.A., D.D., Dean of Ely.
REV. JOHN THOMSON, Minister of Howard Congregational Church, Bedford.
REV. L. J. WHITE-THOMSON, M.A., Rector of St. Martin's Church, Canterbury.
REV. WILLIAM JAMES WOODS, B.A., Secretary of Congregational Union of England and Wales (Member of The Pilgrimage Reception Committee).

Contents of The Book of The Pilgrimage

	PAGE
DAY BY DAY ITINERARY	11
COMMITTEES . . .	14
OUR PILGRIMAGE — *Editorials from The Congregationalist*	17
OUR PILGRIMS — *Editorials from The Congregationalist*	20
BON VOYAGE — *Dr. DeWitt S. Clark*	23
PILGRIMS — A POEM — *Mrs. Harriet Prescott Spofford*	26
ON THE OCEAN — *Dr. A. E. Dunning*	27
PILGRIMS IN PLYMOUTH — *Miss F. J. Dyer*	31
PILGRIMS IN EXETER — *Miss F. J. Dyer*	37
PILGRIMS IN WELLS AND GLASTONBURY — *Miss F. J. Dyer*	41
PILGRIMS IN SALISBURY AND BEMERTON — *Miss F. J. Dyer*	49
PILGRIMS IN WINCHESTER AND FARNHAM — *Miss F. J. Dyer* . . .	54
PILGRIMS IN OXFORD AND CAMBRIDGE — *Miss F. J. Dyer*	64
PILGRIMS IN BEDFORD — *Miss F. J. Dyer*	72
PILGRIMS IN LONDON AND REIGATE — *Miss F. J. Dyer* . .	78

Contents of The Book of The Pilgrimage

PILGRIMS IN CANTERBURY — *Miss F. J. Dyer*	89
PILGRIMS IN BOSTON — *Miss F. J. Dyer* . .	95
PILGRIMS IN LINCOLN — *Miss F. J. Dyer*	98
PILGRIMS IN PILGRIM LAND — *Miss F. J. Dyer*	102
SCROOBY, BAWTRY, AUSTERFIELD, GAINSBOROUGH.	
PILGRIMS IN ELY — *Miss F. J. Dyer* . .	117
PILGRIMS IN NORWICH — *Miss F. J. Dyer*	121
PILGRIMS IN HOLLAND — *Miss F. J. Dyer*	129
LOOKING BACKWARD — *Miss Dyer and other Members of the Party* .	139
A WORD ABOUT THE CLOSING DAYS — *Dr. A. E. Dunning*	146
PILGRIMAGE PERSPECTIVES — *Rev. Sherrod Soule and Mr. Albert Dawson* .	148

WITH THE INITIAL LETTER OF EACH CHAPTER Mr. Ipsen, the artist, has incorporated a characteristic sketch. A word of explanation regarding some of them will not be out of place: The initial design for the Plymouth chapter shows the official Seal; Exeter, one of the Transeptal Towers of the Cathedral; Wells, inverted tower arch in the Cathedral; Salisbury, gateway of the Cathedral Close; Winchester, stairway of the Keep at Farnham Castle; Oxford and Cambridge, Seals of Mansfield and Immanuel Colleges; Bedford, Bunyan's Chair; London, Houses of Parliament; Canterbury, Norman stairway in the Cathedral Close; Boston, cells in the Basement of the Old Town Hall; Lincoln, "The Imp" in the Angel Choir of the Cathedral; Pilgrim Land, interior of Austerfield Church; Ely, the Cathedral Coat of Arms; Norwich, Pulls Ferry at the bottom of the Cathedral Close.

Day by Day Itinerary
ENGLAND.

June 11 (Thursday). 8 A.M. Arrive at Plymouth. P.M. Government Dockyards. The Hoe, etc.

June 12 (Friday). A.M. Inspection of the historic sights of Plymouth under the guidance of the borough librarian. 7.30 P.M. Reception by the Mayor in the Guildhall.

June 13 (Saturday). Excursion by Steamer (chartered by the Evangelical Free Church Council) to Mount Edgcumbe, by permission of the Earl of Mount Edgcumbe, P.C. 4 P.M. Depart. 5.54 P.M. Arrive at Exeter. 6 P.M. The Cathedral, under guidance of Rev. Canon Edmonds. 9 P.M. We come in the Congregational Church.

June 14 (Sunday). In Exeter.

June 15 (Monday). 7.45 A.M. Depart. 11.13 A.M. Arrive at Wells. After luncheon, drive to Glastonbury. Tea at the Congregational Hall. Return to Wells to sleep.

June 16 (Tuesday). 7.30 A.M. Depart. 10.04 A.M. Arrive at Salisbury. Welcome and Breakfast in the Congregational Hall. 12. The Cathedral, under the guidance of the Sub-Dean (Rev. Dr. Bourne). 2.30 P.M. Bemerton and Sarum. 4.15 P.M. Depart. 5.43 P.M. Arrive at Winchester. The Cathedral. 9 P.M. Welcome in the British Hall.

June 17 (Wednesday). 9.32 A.M. Depart. 10.40 A.M. Arrive at Farnham. 1 P.M. Luncheon in Farnham Castle, by invitation of the Lord Bishop of Winchester. 2.26 P.M. Depart. 3.42 P.M. Arrive at Winchester. Holy Cross Hospital and Winchester School. 5.45 P.M. Depart. 8.28 P.M. Arrive at Oxford.

June 18 (Thursday). Round of the Colleges. 1.30 P.M. Luncheon at Mansfield College; Address by Principal Fairbairn.

June 19 (Friday). 7.50 A.M. Depart. 9.33 A.M. Arrive at Bedford. Breakfast at Elstow; Address in the Moot Hall by Dr. John Brown. The Church, Bunyan's Cottage, etc. Luncheon at Bunyan Meeting, Bedford. Tea at Howard Memorial Church. 5.41 P.M. Depart. 7.50 P.M. Arrive at London. Hotel Cecil.

June 20 (Saturday). A.M. Drive about London. 4 P.M. Garden Party at "The Firs," Clarence Road, Clapham Park, by invitation of Halley Stewart, Esq., J.P., in connection with the 250th anniversary of Clapham Congregational Church (Dr. Guinness Rogers).

June 21 (Sunday). In London.

June 22 (Monday). 9 A.M. Excursion to Canterbury. Greeting in Congregational Church. St. Martin's. 1.30 P.M. At the Deanery Address by Dean Farrar. The Cathedral, under guidance of Dean Farrar and Canon Scott-Robinson. 3 P.M. Service in Cathedral. Return to London. 8 P.M. "The Sign of the Cross."

June 23 (Tuesday). 2.30 P.M. St. Paul's Cathedral, under guidance of the Archdeacon of London (Ven. Dr. Sinclair). 4 P.M. Short Choral Service. Tea in the Chapter House, by invitation of the Archdeacon. 5 P.M. Reception at Memorial Hall.

June 24 (Wednesday). A.M. Breakfast at The Priory, Reigate, as guests of Lady Henry Somerset. By Thames Steamboat to Tower, etc. 2.45 P.M. Assemble in Choir of the Abbey for Service at 3 P.M. After service, Address in the Jerusalem Chamber by the Dean (Very Rev. Dr. Bradley). 6 P.M. Tea at Christ Church, Westminster Bridge Road, by invitation of Rev. F. B. Meyer, B.A., and Dr. Newman Hall.

June 25 (Thursday). 2.30 P.M. Depart. 3.54 P.M. Arrive at Cambridge. 5 P.M. Garden Party at Edenfield, by invitation of Mr. and Mrs. Munsey.

June 26 (Friday). 9.30 A.M. Meet at Dr. Forsyth's Church. Mr. A. W. W. Dale and other friends conduct round the Colleges, etc.

June 27 (Saturday). 10.06 A.M. Depart. 11.58 A.M. Arrive at Boston. Luncheon at the Peacock, the Mayor presiding. St. Botolph's Church. 3.30 P.M. Depart. 4.42 P.M. Arrive at Lincoln. 8 P.M. Welcome in County Assembly Room.

June 28 (Sunday). In Lincoln.

Day by Day Itinerary

June 29 (Monday). 7.30 A.M. Depart. 8.20 A.M. Arrive at Scrooby. Drive to Bawtry, Austerfield, Gainsborough. 1.30 P.M. Luncheon in Gainsborough Old Hall (formerly the Residence of the Lords of the Manor, and in which the Separatist Church of 1602 was probably organized), by permission of the Lord of the Manor (Sir Hickman B. Bacon, Bart.). 3 P.M. Stone-laying of John Robinson Memorial Church by Hon. T. F. Bayard, Chairman, Rev. J. Morlais Jones. Speakers, Dr. Mackennal and Rev. Morton Dexter. 5 P.M. Tea in Public Hall. 8 P.M. Mass Meeting in Wesley Chapel. Chairman, Albert Spicer, Esq., M.P. Speakers, Dr. Rogers, Dr. C. A. Berry, Dr. Park, and Dr. Richardson.

June 30 (Tuesday). A.M. Lincoln Cathedral, under guidance of the Sub-Dean. 2.33 P.M. Depart. 4.18 P.M. Arrive at Ely. 5 P.M. Tea at the Deanery, by invitation of the Dean (Very Rev. Dr. Stubbs). 9.10 P.M. Moonlight Organ and Violin Recital in the Cathedral, arranged by the Dean.

July 1 (Wednesday). 8.47 A.M. Depart. 10.33 A.M. Arrive at Norwich. 11 A.M. Service in the Cathedral (800th Anniversary). Preacher, the Lord Archbishop of Armagh. 1 P.M. Luncheon, by invitation of the Dean (Very Rev. Dr. Lefroy). 4.30 P.M. Garden Party at Carrow House, by invitation of J. J. Colman, Esq. 8 P.M. Public Meeting in Old Meeting House.

July 2 (Thursday). Norwich. The Castle, Guildhall, Dr. Barrett's Church, Curat House, etc. 6.03 P.M. Depart. 8.37 P.M. Arrive at Harwich; embark for Holland.

HOLLAND AND THE CONTINENT.

July 3 (Friday). 8 A.M. Arrive at Rotterdam. Carriages to Delfshaven, where the Pilgrims embarked for Plymouth. Return to Rotterdam for luncheon. Visit the house of Erasmus, Boyman's Museum, and other places of interest. Afternoon train to The Hague. Evening, a concert at Scheveningen.

July 4 (Saturday). At The Hague. Visit the picture gallery, the Gevangenpoort, and other points. Celebration of Independence Day at Hotel Paulez, with addresses by members of the party. Evening train to Leiden.

July 5 (Sunday). 2 P.M. Service in the house standing on the spot where John Robinson once lived, sermon by Dr. Alexander Mackennal. Visit the University buildings and gardens. 6 P.M. Christian Endeavor service at the Hotel.

July 6 (Monday). Morning train to Haarlem. Special organ recital at the Groote Kerk. Visit the Museum and other places of interest. 1 P.M. Train to Amsterdam, Hotel Victoria.

July 7 (Tuesday). Morning carriage drive to the royal palace, the principal Jewish synagogue and about the city. Afternoon, by steamboat through the canals, visit the Ryks Museum and Zoölogical Gardens.

July 8 (Wednesday). By chartered steamer to Broek, visiting some of the model Dutch farmhouses. Luncheon at Monnikendam. Pass through Edam to the Island of Marken in the Zuyder Zee. Return to Amsterdam in the evening.

July 9 (Thursday). Visit the street of the Brownists and the house once occupied by the Pilgrims, the remainder of the day spent according to individual preferences.

July 10 (Friday). Excursion by chartered steamer to Alkmaar, visiting the cheese market, the Church of St. Lawrence, etc. Return by way of Zaandam, visiting the house once occupied by Peter the Great.

July 11 (Saturday). 9.10 A.M. Depart for Cologne. Arrive 3 P.M. Visit the Cathedral and Church of St. Ursula.

July 12 (Sunday). A.M. Attend the cathedral services. P.M. Christian Endeavor service in the parlors of the Hotel Victoria.

July 13 (Monday). The entire day spent on the Rhine, from Cologne to Mayence.

July 14 (Tuesday). 9 A.M. Depart from Mayence. Arrive in Heidelberg about 11 A.M. Drive through the town and to the castle. 3 P.M. By train to Baden-Baden. Evening, concert at the Kursaal.

July 15 (Wednesday). By morning train through the Black Forest. 7 P.M. Arrive at Zürich.

July 16 (Thursday). In Zürich. Visit the Cathedral, the collection of antiquities, and other places of interest. By afternoon train to Arth, whence the ascent of the Rigi is made. Final gathering of the party, with addresses, in the Red Parlor of the Rigi Kulm Hotel.

July 17 (Friday). Descend by rail to Vitznau, whence the boat is taken across the Lake of the Four Cantons to Lucerne. Here the party separate, twenty-one members taking a tour through Switzerland, others going direct to Paris, still others leaving for various parts of Europe.

REV. ALEXANDER MACKENNAL, D.D.,
Chairman of the Co-operating Committee, in charge of the arrangements for the reception of the Party in England.

The American Committee

Appointed by the National Council of Congregational Churches (Syracuse, 1895) to represent the Council in connection with the arrangements for The Pilgrimage

Rev. C. R. PALMER, D.D., Bridgeport, Ct., *Chairman.*

Hon. E. W. BLATCHFORD, Chicago, Ill.
Rev. NEHEMIAH BOYNTON, D.D., Boston, Mass.
Rev. A. H. BRADFORD, D.D., Montclair, N. J.
Hon. LYMAN BREWSTER, Danbury, Ct.
Hon. S. B. CAPEN, Boston, Mass.

Rev. MORTON DEXTER, Boston, Mass.
Rev. A. E. DUNNING, D.D., Boston, Mass.
Rev. G. E. HALL, D.D., Dover, N. H.
Rev. W. A. ROBINSON, D.D., Middletown, N. Y.
Pres. C. F. THWING, D.D., Cleveland, O.

The English Co=operating Committee

In charge of the arrangements for the reception of the party in England

Rev. ALEXANDER MACKENNAL, D.D., Bowdon, *Chairman.*

Rev. G. S. BARRETT, D.D., Norwich.
Rev. C. A. BERRY, D.D., Wolverhampton.
Rev. JOHN BROWN, D.D., Bedford.
ALBERT DAWSON, Esq., London, *Secretary.*
Rev. R. F. HORTON, D.D., Hampstead, London.

Rev. ANDREW MEARNS, Secretary of the London Congregational Union.
Rev. J. G. ROGERS, D.D., Clapham, London.
Rev. WILLIAM J. WOODS, B.A., Secretary of the Congregational Union of England and Wales.

Rev. J. G. Rogers, D.D.

Rev. G. S. Barrett, D.D.

Rev. John Brown, D.D.

Rev. Andrew Mearns

Rev. A. Mackennal, D.D.

Rev. W. T. Woods, B.A.

Rev. C. A. Berry, D.D.

Rev. R. F. Horton, D.D.

Albert Dawson, Esq.

THE ENGLISH CO-OPERATING COMMITTEE.

A. E. DUNNING — Editor
W. F. WHITTEMORE — Publisher
ALBERT DAWSON — London Editor

"The Staff of THE CONGREGATIONALIST specially concerned in the Management of The Pilgrimage."

Our Pilgrimage

THE first public announcement, with full details, of the purpose of *The Congregationalist* to undertake the historic tour described in the following pages appeared in an editorial with the above title under date of October 24, 1895. It said:—

The Congregationalist's tour to the Orient, beginning early in the present year, much exceeded the anticipations of its projectors. It gave to the members of the party greater advantages, both of education and recreation, than they expected, and it interested many thousands of our readers in historical matters of great importance to their spiritual life.

Encouraged by this success, the proprietors of *The Congregationalist* have been for some time preparing for next summer a pilgrimage to scenes of historic interest in England and Holland. The plan of this journey, which was briefly announced in connection with the Oriental Tour, has been for some years in mind with a view to creating greater interest in Congregational history and strengthening ties of fellowship between Congregationalists in America and in the mother country. The suggestion of it last summer in England brought at once the most cordial response from leaders of our denomination there, who expressed their willingness to act in coöperation with brethren on this side of the Atlantic. Nor was it confined to Congregationalists. The Dean of Canterbury, Dr. Farrar, has extended a hearty invitation to the American pilgrims to visit that cathedral and city, rich in historic associations. Other like invitations, we are assured, will be given as soon as our plans are definitely announced. The National Council has appointed several representative clergymen and laymen to visit Gainsborough in connection with the party, in the expectation that that church, closely associated with the beginnings of Congregationalism, will by that time have its building ready for dedication. It is also expected that the representatives of the council will participate in the celebration of the 250th anniversary of the Clapham Church (Dr. J. Guinness Rogers) in London.

The Congregationalist has made arrangements for the party to sail from New York, June 4, in one of the express steamers of the Hamburg-American Line, and has prepared an itinerary of places to be visited. It is expected that the tour will occupy two months. The number will be limited to the accommodations engaged. This pilgrimage is not to be an excursion merely for sight-seeing, but the party is intended to include a company of representative Congregationalists, men and women, interested in the history of Congregationalism and of the movements which

The Book of the Pilgrimage

led to the settlement of New England. For this reason we have engaged accommodations on express steamers so as to economize time as well as promote comfort, and the arrangements for the entire journey will be on a broad and liberal scale. It is probable that a similar company will be organized in England to unite with the American party, and it is certain that every facility will be afforded for acquaintance with scenes of greatest historic interest to be visited, and with persons prominent in our denomination and in other churches in England and Holland. The season has been chosen when the countries to be visited are most attractive and when the pleasures of travel are greatest. While the regular trip includes a journey up the Rhine, a brief sojourn in Switzerland and France, arrangements are being made by which members of the party may extend their travel if they wish. We believe we have provided for as interesting and profitable a journey as is possible for those to whom such a pilgrimage appeals.

On the date of sailing, June 4, there were two more editorials, one of which said in part : —

We are aware that the special company which is setting sail this week on the Columbia for England and Holland is only one of many groups of travelers who will this summer cross the Atlantic and wander hither and thither in the Old World. But a distinctiveness is given to this *Congregationalist* Pilgrimage in the special object it has in view, in the composition of the party, and in the degree of interest which the undertaking has aroused in this country and abroad.

Believing that kindred tastes and sympathies are the only conditions that make travel with others endurable and profitable, and believing, too, that journeys to certain historic shrines can be made most advantageously in a party carefully made up and wisely directed, we have provided such an opportunity. The response as respects the English Pilgrimage has been no less gratifying than that accorded the Oriental Tour. Indeed, the party which sails this week is larger by ten than the company who went to the Holy Land.

The principle of associated travel is being widely recognized. Boston will soon send across the Atlantic representatives of one of its oldest military organizations to gain by their journey and by contact with its London prototype a larger impetus toward patriotism. Every summer sees many larger or smaller companies of persons whose common interest in scholarly or scientific pursuits forms a delightful bond of union as they move about in the Old World together. It has seemed to us but a further extension of this idea to organize a party of our Congregational people whose unifying tie should be a genuine regard for the historic side of their faith. We have not been disappointed in our expectation, for the size of the Pilgrimage but faintly measures the attention which the project has secured, and could all go who have expressed a desire to be numbered among the pilgrims it would take more than one ship of the size of the Columbia to carry them.

We feel confident that the individual members of the party will have occasion

Our Pilgrimage

many times to realize what special advantages association with it secures. Doors will be opened which do not usually swing inwards to the touch of the tourist; opportunities to become acquainted with the leaders in our own denomination and with prominent ecclesiastics of the Church of England will be frequent and rewarding, while the exchange of friendly greetings and the giving and receiving of courtesies must surely promote a better understanding between hosts and guests and thus cement the ties between England and America. We have not overstated the warmth of anticipation with which our English brethren look forward to the coming of this American delegation, and we are glad to be able to gather such a representative group of our own people and put them in close touch, not merely with the soil and buildings that are sacred in our eyes, but with the men and the forces that are helping to upbuild and regenerate modern England. As we signalized the beginning of our eightieth year of existence as a paper by conducting a party to the Holy Land, so we are fittingly concluding our eightieth birthday celebration by sending forth these pilgrims to England and Holland.

Through letters from the different members of our staff included in the party we shall hear, from week to week, with reference to its doings and its varied delights. Meanwhile we voice the kind feeling and large hopes of all of our readers when we wish the outgoing pilgrims a safe and smooth passage, good fellowship among themselves, invigoration of body and spirit, and on sea and land an ever deepening sense of God's protection and of the beauty and richness of the world which he has created and adorned for his children's use and enjoyment.

Our Pilgrims

ANOTHER editorial in *The Congregationalist* of June 4 dwelt more particularly on certain personal facts and characteristics, and thus served as a letter of introduction to such of the pilgrims as had no acquaintance with each other before leaving America. It said : —

A national character is given to the party by the fact that ten States are represented in its membership. Naturally New England furnishes the largest proportion, there being several representatives from each of the four States of New Hampshire, Massachusetts, Rhode Island, and Connecticut, the old Bay State being in the van, as would be expected, since the party was organized in Boston. New York State furnishes half a dozen pilgrims; others are from Pennsylvania, Illinois, Iowa, Arkansas, and California.

There is also a good variety in the vocations of the different pilgrims. Such a trip as has been planned appeals, of course, particularly to ministers and students, but professional and business men generally have also shown a desire to participate in it. The dozen or more ministers are nearly all pastors in active service, and it is noticeable that many of them have rendered exceptionally long service in their present fields. Their prospective rest and enjoyment will be all the more keenly relished because of the consciousness of having rendered to their people faithful and unwearying service for so many years. They in turn, in one or two cases at least, have facilitated the proposed trip by such substantial assistance as pastors well established in the affections of their flocks from time to time receive.

The clergymen of the party will not have it all their own way, by any means, for three business men, a lawyer, a general, a physician, and a school teacher will introduce a considerable flavor of other callings.

Without attempting to particularize as respects the *personnel* of the party, there will be general interest in a word or two with reference to certain of its members. Rev. W. E. Park, D.D., bears a name honored on both sides of the sea. He is a son of the eminent theologian still living quietly at Andover, and possesses many of those strong and gracious qualities which are associated with his father. He has been pastor at Gloversville, N. Y., for the last twenty years, and in the State and national assemblies of our order, as well as in many lines of public life, he has taken a prominent and useful part. Another New York pastor, Rev. W. A. Robinson, D.D., of Middletown, is a direct descendant of that pioneer Congregationalist, John Robinson, and in his turn has found a large place of service and made an individual

Our Pilgrims

reputation. When a pastor in Vermont he was for three years on the State Board of Education, and he was a member of the Constitutional Convention of 1870. He was president of the Home Missionary Board of New York State in 1884, and his twenty years' pastorate at Homer was as fruitful as it was exceptional.

Probably the oldest member of the delegation is Rev. Edward Robie, of Greenland, N. H., still in the harness there, though it is forty-four years since he was installed. His tastes are scholarly, and a country parish has permitted him to cultivate them to such good purpose that Dartmouth College some time ago bestowed the honor of a Doctorate of Divinity upon him, which, however, he was so modest as to refuse, though subsequently persuaded to accept the honor.

Another New Hampshire minister is Rev. Cyrus Richardson, D.D., of Nashua, an excellent preacher and pastor, one of the pillars of Granite State Congregationalism and a trustee of Dartmouth College. Rev. W. W. Leete, though of Eastern origin and training, is one of the most popular and successful ministers in Illinois. Rev. L. L. Wirt has been for several years the efficient superintendent of the Sunday-school interests of our denomination in California. Rev. Messrs. F. D. Sargent, R. P. Hibbard, E. K. Holden, and Sherrod Soule have charge of important churches.

Hon. Jonathan A. Lane is a typical Boston merchant, representing in his birth, tastes, training, and influence all that is best, and standing high in the commercial circles of the city, and of the nation as well. For many years he was president of the Boston Merchants Association. He has been active in politics and has exhibited an uncommon amount of public spirit in many directions. He is one of the leading members of Union Church.

Gen. Elbert Wheeler, a graduate of West Point, has been inspector-general upon the staff of three New Hampshire governors, one of whom once said: "If all military men who belong to the Church were like General Wheeler, the Church would shine in the world." Dr. A. S. Wallace is the leading physician of Nashua and a patriotic and high-minded gentleman. Mr. C. H. Noyes, also from Nashua, is a teacher in its high school. Mr. N. W. Littlefield is a prominent lawyer of Providence, R. I.

The ladies of the party are no less deserving of particular mention, but we will now allude only to Miss A. F. Burnham, of Cambridge, who is the editor of the juvenile grade of lessons and Sunday-school papers issued by the Congregational Sunday-School and Publishing Society, and of which many hundreds of thousands are sold, and to Miss Dyer, the editor of the Home Department of *The Congregationalist*. Many of the gentlemen are accompanied by their wives, and the party includes a group of women prominent in Hartford social and religious circles.

Most, if not all, of the pilgrims have pronounced Puritan and Congregational sympathies, and without undervaluing the general pleasure inhering in such a trip as this, they look upon it as a means of education such as is not often available. They will doubtless find much pleasure in one another's society. They are certainly a

The Book of the Pilgrimage

delegation which will fitly represent American Congregationalism, and they will bring back from the shrines which they visit in England a larger understanding of historic Congregationalism, of its heroes of other years and its present-day exponents.

Mrs. Harriet Prescott Spofford, a gifted contributor to *The Congregationalist*, sent us "athwart the foaming brine" to the music of her verse in the poem printed on page 26, and Rev. De Witt S. Clark, of Salem, Mass., a member of the Oriental party, gave us his farewell in a little classic, entitled "Bon Voyage," which is worthy a prominent place in the chronicles of The Book of the Pilgrimage.

Members of The Pilgrimage

Miss Lucy A. Brainard, Hartford, Ct.
Miss Fanny F. Brown, Hartford, Ct.
Miss Anna F. Burnham, Cambridge, Mass.
Miss Ellen M. Case, Hartford, Ct.
Rev. Morton Dexter, Boston, Mass.
Rev. A. E. Dunning, D.D., Boston, Mass.
Mrs. A. E. Dunning, Boston, Mass.
Miss Emily B. Dunning, Boston, Mass.
Miss Frances J. Dyer, Boston, Mass.
Miss Carrie M. Galpin, New Haven, Ct.
Mrs. Arthur L. Goodrich, Hartford, Ct.
Rev. Rufus P. Hibbard, Gloucester, Mass.
Rev. Edwin K. Holden, Bridgeport, Ct.
Mrs. Carrie A. Hyde, Hartford, Ct.
Hon. Jonathan A. Lane, Boston, Mass.
Rev. William White Leete, Rockford, Ill.
Mr. Charles Liffler, Jr., Boston, Mass.
Mrs. Charles Liffler, Jr., Boston, Mass.
Mr. Nathan W. Littlefield, Providence, R. I.
Mrs. Nathan W. Littlefield, Providence, R. I.
Miss Mary J. McAdoo, North Bloomfield, O.
Mr. Charles H. Noyes, Nashua, N. H.
Rev. William E. Park, D.D., Gloversville, N. Y.

Miss Mary E. Pierce, Whitman, Mass.
Miss E. M. Pomeroy, Reading, Pa.
Mrs. Charles N. Prouty, Spencer, Mass.
Miss Marion R. Prouty, Spencer, Mass.
Miss Emily Peirce Rand, Taunton, Mass.
Rev. Cyrus Richardson, D.D., Nashua, N. H.
Rev. Edward Robie, D.D., Greenland, N. H.
Miss L. E. Robie, Greenland, N. H.
Rev. William A. Robinson, D.D., Middletown, N.Y.
Mrs. William A. Robinson, Middletown, N. Y.
Miss Harriet Rowell, Hartford, Ct.
Rev. Frank D. Sargent, Putnam, Ct.
J. Stephen Scott, D.D.S., Boston, Mass.
Mrs. Minnie Scott, Lamar, Ark.
Miss L. E. Seymour, Bristol, Ct.
Rev. Sherrod Soule, Naugatuck, Ct.
Mr. O. C. Starrett, Sheldon, Ia.
Mrs. R. M. Storrs, Brooklyn, N. Y.
A. S. Wallace, M.D., Nashua, N. H.
Mrs. John S. West, Tiverton, R. I.
Gen. Elbert Wheeler, Nashua, N. H.
Mr. William F. Whittemore, Boston, Mass.
Rev. Loyal L. Wirt, San Francisco, Cal.

Rev. Alexander Mackennal, D.D., Bowdon, Eng.
Miss Effie Mackennal, Bowdon, Eng.
Rev. E. J. Dukes, Bridgewater, Eng.
Mr. George Hardy, London, Eng.
Mr. W. R. Wright, London, Eng.

Bon Voyage

PERHAPS we ought to say "Bon Pilgrimage!" since the voyage is but a small part of the anticipated experience of *The Congregationalist's* party setting out for "Old World Shrines." Yet the voyage comes first, as you are likely to discover. Fortunate are you that it is to be made on that splendid ship so worthy by name and appointment to convey back to the mother country the sons and daughters of them who so long ago — as we Americans count the years — came over the sea for God and freedom of conscience' sake, to plant Congregationalism on these virgin shores.

"Time brings in his revenges." Now there is welcome at cathedral, university, and Guildhall doors to the schismatics, whom once the king and ecclesiastic would "harry out of the land." Would that we all might go and receive the meed of justice, so long delayed, from British lips and hands! Would we all were among the elect who again, as at the first, have been "sifted out of a continent" by *The Congregationalist* patent mesh for this joy and honor! Alas! as in politics, the choice does not fall on us! It is the other man who is called and we are invited to offer him our congratulations.

This we do heartily, universally: "All the saints salute you." We are told there are in your company all sorts and conditions of Congregationalists — lawyers, teachers, merchants, physicians, ministers, and some women, possibly of the "new" variety, of course no *old*. We tremble at the thought of these "falling out by the way," and so repeat the Josephic admonition.

Your leader is no novice in the pilgrimage business. He has conducted already a considerable band into the very presence of Rameses the Great and to the Holy City itself. He knows what labors, dangers, and sufferings are involved in the task He can curb the rash, cheer the faint, bear with the grumbler, and command when he must.

His "sesame" has the magic charm to open many places closed to the curious traveler, and lords and bishops and lackeys do him homage, for his is a prevailing name. His is the habit of getting things, Dun. He can speak, discreetly as Solomon, on any topic, from Dutch currency to higher criticism, or the best specifics against heresy or seasickness. By the way, we advise you to leave "brush remedies" to the cats, and take your tossing and qualms in that heroic Christian spirit they did on the Mayflower The "Gem of the Ocean" will do as little in the way of upsetting you as any craft, even if you do not have a gimbal-hung stateroom. You need not hesitate at every chance to lay in one of the Columbia's square meals. Show to the cynical worldlings how "powerful them pious cats."

Then to the daily promenade, the stirring strains of the orchestra, the dozing in the hired chair, the "light reading," the plowing through fog banks to the cheerful toot of the whistle, the excitement of a passing "liner," the noisy laugh over antique stories, and the first sighting of Albion's chalky cliffs — how we all would like to share in these!

So you are really going — by way of the Establishment premises — to see where noble and simple ideals first germinated in true souls! Scrooby and Austerfield are to unfold their secrets to you. No grandeur of Exeter and Wells and Salisbury is to persuade you that it is better to "enrich" your "service" after the church pattern. As psalm singers and lovers of unrobed ministers and white window glass and hard pews, you, Puritans and Pilgrims, are now to offer your silent protests against all that is spectacular in worship; to "kiss" no "calves" of abominations, parading in the name of religion, though all do it over there. Remember the eyes of a denomination are on you as faithful witnesses. May you be equal to the test!

Neither are you to inveigh against strange customs and silly rules. We shall expect you all to remember to say "carriage" and "lift" and "tram" and "tuppence" and "boots" and "tarts," and never let slip a Yankee "guess." They didn't at Brewster's house or Bunyan's cottage.

London is to receive, amaze, and weary you by its endless stretches of monotonous streets, historic buildings, and oppressive problems. You won't solve all the latter, but don't try to *do* the British Museum, or to remember all the inscriptions on the monuments in the Abbey. Leave something for the next time, or there won't be any next time.

Breakfasts is the name of them — those semi-gustatory, semi-oratorical receptions, of which we learn you are to have your fill. "Go to, let us have a breakfast," will be the first serious proposition we shall hear on your return. Philanthropy is in it and culture and creature benefit. The Puritans will have all the needed salt in themselves.

Our dear Congregational appendix — our "proselyte of the gate" at Oxford! How proud you will be as you walk about it and count its neo-classic towers, with never a rook condescending to make its nest in them! We all join in any hurrahs with which you may rashly break the dignified silence of that cloistered retreat. We do not care if you wake Wolsey from his sleep to see how the Protestant thrives where he was once anathematized and burned. As you journey, in true Pilgrim fashion, to the tomb of Becket, not on palfrey and prancing steed, but via the London and Southwestern Railroad, we enjoin you to reserve, every one, your "Canterbury tale" till we can have it at first hand. We empower you to contribute our Peter's Pence for the restoration of the ancient fane, as our good friend, the Dean, cordially invites all generous Americans to do.

Bon Voyage

Across the yeasty stretch of waters, in the realm of flaunting windmills and piles of red cannon-ball cheeses, clatter of sabots and jingle of guldens, how will you survive, unless by the same honest hearts as the first fugitives did! Settle it for us, whether our fathers were more Dutchmen than Englishmen. If you can get any more "light" from John Robinson on that matter, bottle it and let it "break forth" on arrival here. We rejoice that you cannot stay long there, lest your morals suffer in the corrupt atmosphere as did those of the Pilgrim youth. Paris the gay, and Heidelberg the romantic, and Lucerne the beautiful — the names make us almost wild with desire to set foot within their borders. Some, with a preference for H^2O, still find it desirable to drink "the wine of the country," but, brethren, "we are persuaded better things of you, though we thus speak."

Sunrises on the Righi, castles on the Rhine, the mysterious concoctions of the *table d'hôte*, these crowd upon our imagination till envy stirs within us and we crack some of the commandments. This is our consolation — soon the days will have passed and you will be handed like the Star of Empire a rested, wise, enthusiastic band of travelers, who have done what you could to seal more firmly the bonds which unite Briton and American, and to bring in the everlasting years of peace and the latter-day glory of our Congregational order. So we say to the good ship Columbia,

> Sail on, nor fear to breast the sea!
> Our hearts, our hopes, are all with thee,
> . . . .
> Are all with thee — are all with thee.

Sincerely yours,
D E Waldclaw

Pilgrims

Memories of men of long ago, on the Old Barbican make your round,
Come from your unhorizoned home and welcome your children to Plymouth Sound !
For who are these that fly as a cloud, and as the doves to their windows fly,
After them blowing the wild west wind, over them springing the western sky?

After them curling the long green wave, over them blowing the salt sea spray,
O Pilgrims who sailed off into the gale, Pilgrims adventure back to-day,
Bringing the fruit of all your faith, bringing the answer to all your prayers,
For your primal hope and your conquering dream, finished, invincible, crowned, is theirs !

Now on this pleasanter pilgrimage than of scallop-shell and staff and shoon,
Roving the vale of Avalon, blossomy, bowery, green with June,
With them, great Memories, haply tread the dust of Arthur, your ancient peer,
And linger above George Herbert's grave for the gathered flower or the dropping tear.

Go with them where a Pilgrim made his earlier progress o'er hill and dale,
And tell them the awful scope and sweep of the dream that was dreamed in Bedford Jail,
Till the far Celestial City's shine into the dusky prison fell,
And all the Delectable Country's air blew its breath through the narrow cell.

Where Chaucer his pilgrims led before, lead your children, great spirits, now !
Man of a people who curbed a king, Becket shall smooth his angry brow,
From his heaven of poesy and song, Milton shall stoop in mighty gyre,
And the men shall come to companion you whose souls for their faith went up in fire.

Down shadowy length of cloistered aisles, dim with a glory of blazoned dyes,
Where vast processional pillars lift the vaulted roof into underskies,
Where the tide of music falls away from fretted stone and from sculpture fair,
Show them the splendor you thought less worth than the blessed freedom of simple prayer !

And turn, when the English twilight falls like a blessing given at day's surcease,
With the singing sway of ancestral boughs and the passing fragrance of dewy peace,
And tell them with what heart-breaking love these happy fallows and fields you trod,
And left them, that those who followed you might come close, close to the heart of God !

Most cordially Ever,
Harriet P. Spofford

On the Ocean

NEW YORK harbor was brilliant with sunshine on the morning of June 4, when promptly at seven o'clock the steamer Columbia moved out of her dock and pointed her prow toward England. Among her three hundred and forty cabin passengers were *The Congregationalist's* pilgrims bound for Old-World shrines. The great ship moved triumphant in the midst of the busy scene, past craft of every sort, till the tall buildings of the great cities gave place to green shores and beside them flotillas of vessels with white sails swaying idly above a glassy sea.

Soon we moved out into the solemn silences of the deep, where the splendid ship, with her broad decks covered with a gay company, seemed an intrusion. Yet to the talk and laughter came no answer other than constant smiles from sea and sky. Some, however, too soon grew tired of the monotony of the summer stillness and wished the wind might blow. They had their wish. Fog and rain and rolling waves drove the

Hamburg-American Steamship Columbia.

amateur travelers to their staterooms and to meditations which frequently broke forth in audible renunciation of possessions too eagerly received, too briefly held. The blow was a short one and mercifully light. Sunday afternoon a fine audience gathered to listen to a helpful sermon from Bishop Potter of New York, from Ps. 139:4. The bishop told the company of travelers from their homes to foreign lands that though they might escape the cares of business, two things would remain with them — the consciousness of self and the consciousness of God. Our highest

The Book of the Pilgrimage

dignity is to accept gladly the responsibilities which God places on us through our gifts and opportunities.

A journey across the Atlantic in these days offers little of interest to the general public, and this one would not deserve mention here were it not for the company of pilgrims gathered by *The Congregationalist* to celebrate its eightieth year by visiting scenes familiar in the history of New England. These pilgrims, too, were described quite at length in our paper before leaving America, but many items of interest have come out in the conversations daily held on the steamer's decks. Two names, at least, are borne by direct descendants of the original Pilgrims, Robinson and Soule. Others, also, can trace their ancestry back to the same source, and some cherish family traditions of brave deeds done in the early days of Massachusetts Colony. One lady relates that among her grandmothers of several generations back one was of the company which became celebrated in the building of the church in Essex. After the timbers were raised, the town of Ipswich, to which the people belonged, forbade them to proceed, but three of the women mounted their horses, rode to a neighboring settlement, and secured help to finish the building. The three women were imprisoned for a week, when they said they were sorry and were therefore released, but they gained their church and settled a minister. Another lady can trace her ancestry directly back to John and Priscilla Alden.

Captain H. Vogelgesang, SS. Columbian

A Snapshot at Bishop Potter.

Nearly all our pilgrims are of New England blood, but their homes to-day stretch from the Atlantic to the Pacific coast, and not a few of their families have done noble service in planting and maintaining Christian institutions of the Pilgrim type in the interior and far Western States. From others generous gifts have come to Congregational churches, colleges, and seminaries. It would have been difficult to gather so large a company more

On the Ocean

thoroughly identified with interests dear to the denomination which the Pilgrims from old England represented and for which they braved the terrors of the wilderness and planted the greatest of the nations.

In mid-ocean each member of the party received an elegantly engraved invitation from the Mayor of Plymouth to a reception in the Guildhall, Friday evening of this week.

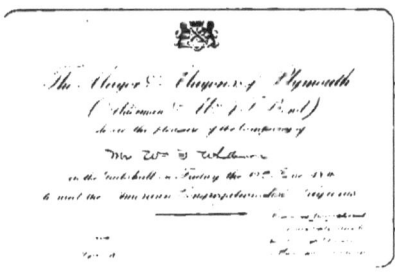

Invitation of the Mayor and Mayoress of Plymouth.

Several of the party seek restoration to health impaired by severe and prolonged labor. It is curious to note how difficult it is for a busy professional or business man to learn the art of being idle. He feels that he must make a business of resting and drive it through. He will sit for a little while in his reclining chair till, impelled by conscience to redeem the time, he paces the deck with Puritan persistence, persuading himself that he is laying up stores of strength for future need. Then he will sit down again and calculate how many more hours he will require to get well. His hardest lesson is to learn that for him idleness is virtue, but nowhere

The Pilgrims, SS. Columbia, mid-ocean.

The Book of the Pilgrimage

are better opportunities to learn that lesson than in a summer voyage like this. The clouds that float lazily in the sky look down with contempt on his restlessness. They clasp hands and steal after the gliding ship and shake themselves over it in summer showers. Then the sun pours his glory over the glinting waves, the band plays dreamy waltzes, the hum of voices falls lower, we close our eyes because the lids grow heavy and wonder how any one can find it difficult to be idle. The end comes all too soon. In just seven days the Columbia discharges us on to a tug at the Plymouth breakwater and majestically moves on toward Hamburg. — *A. E. D.*

SS. Columbia, Plymouth Harbor.

THE BUSINESS ARRANGEMENTS for The Pilgrimage were intrusted to the firm of Henry Gaze & Sons, Ltd., who served us in connection with our Oriental Tour of 1895. They appointed Mr. F. E. Murrell conductor of the party, and he accompanied us throughout the trip. He is a man of unusual executive ability and large experience and managed the affairs of The Pilgrimage to the entire satisfaction of all.

THE SS. COLUMBIA, on which the Pilgrims sailed, is a twin-screw express steamer, built on the Mersey. She is 463 feet long, 55 feet wide, and 35 feet deep from her main deck to the keel, and has five decks constructed solidly of steel and teak. She has two distinct sets of boilers, two engines, two shafts, and two screws, both sets working independently of each other, and separated by one solid longitudinal bulkhead, running from the keel to the upper deck. Each side of the ship is again subdivided into numerous water-tight compartments which do not communicate with each other. The enormous engines of 13,000 horse-power are of the triple-expansive type, and are capable of propelling the ship at the rate of 19½ knots an hour. She has a loading capacity of 7,578 tons, and can carry 220 first cabin passengers, 120 second class, and 800 steerage.

The Pilgrims in Plymouth

MAX O'RELL, in his good-natured criticism of Americans, affirms that they always use adjectives in the superlative degree. But we of *The Congregationalist's* Pilgrimage Party may be pardoned for indulging in superlatives when describing our visit to Plymouth, for our reception there so far exceeded anything we ever dreamed of that moderate speech is impossible. We were met in the Millbay Docks by a deputation of nine gentlemen from the Three Towns' Council of Free Churches, assisted by them through the custom house and escorted to the Duke of Cornwall Hotel. From that time onward, during our three days' stay, they and others were untiring in their attentions, and we shall bring home a new idea of English hospitality.

This committee came out on a tender, and the most sluggish imagination must have been stirred as hosts and guests met in the little cabin to listen to the address of welcome from Rev. Samuel Vincent. What a contrast was our incoming to the outgoing of the Pilgrims of 1620! The sadness

The Hoe, Plymouth.

of their farewell and the joyousness of our welcome, together with the marvelous changes in history since the time of James I, were graphically portrayed by Mr. Vincent in his admirable and cordial speech.

The Book of the Pilgrimage

Plymouth Harbor and Drake's Island from Mount Edgcumbe.

The Pilgrims in Plymouth

The next morning several of this same committee, among them Professor Chapman and Rev. Messrs. Lambert, Rudall, Maxwell, and Slater, accompanied us as we explored the odd nooks and corners of this ancient city of about one hundred thousand inhabitants, under the leadership of the borough librarian, Mr. W. H. K. Wright, who is a Fellow of the Royal Historical Society, an accomplished scholar and an ideal guide. If Americans realized what there is to be seen in Plymouth they would never think of landing at Liverpool or Southampton, now that the American Hamburg steamers touch at this famous port where ships of the admiralty are often at anchor, and where Agnes Weston's remarkable work for British sailors may be seen at the Sailors' Rest.

Rev. J. T. Maxwell.

We went first to the George Street Baptist Chapel, occupying the site of the building in which the Pilgrims were entertained before their departure to America. Among the tablets was one to the memory of Abraham Cheare, a former minister who died in exile on Drake's Island for conscience' sake. The next objective point was St. Andrew's Church, where Archdeacon Wilkinson graciously explained its numerous interesting features, and placed the ancient records at our disposal for examination. We halted at the free library, opposite which stood the town house of Robert Trelawney, one of those to whom James I granted the charter for the founding of the Plymouth Colony. Close by was the residence of Sir Francis Drake,

Memorial Slab and Tablet on The Barbican, Plymouth.

whose statue adorns The Hoe, that fine park on the harbor front. By degrees we came to the Old Barbican pier, passing through the queerest streets and alleys imaginable. No wonder the residents swarmed out of the low, checker-windowed houses to see what the unusual procession meant. Pins Lane and New Street — the latter being the oldest street in town — were indescribably picturesque, with narrow stone steps, similar to those at Clovelly, leading past the diminutive stone cottages, with overhanging second stories, to higher levels beyond. It added much to our enjoyment to be accompanied by John Barrett, the artist, and to hear his comments on these delightfully quaint bits. Of course we all stood on the slab in front of the custom house, inscribed "Mayflower, 1620," and the dozen lineal descendants of the Puritans in our party must have felt a peculiar thrill as their feet touched the sacred stone. The slab and the inscribed tablet affixed to the adjoining wall were placed in their position in 1891, following the meeting of the International Council in London, by Mayor Bond, who, by a happy coincidence, was then serving his first term in office. We passed the house in which Catherine of Aragon was

The Deer Park, Mount Edgcumbe.

entertained by one of the leading merchants in 1501, also the birthplace of Dr. Kitto, now occupied by a brewery, and finished the forenoon by climbing to the top of the old citadel which commands a superb view of the harbor. The old sculptured gateway which forms the main entrance to the citadel rewarded careful examination, and the whole place bristles with stirring incidents connected with the civil wars.

In this connection I wish to voice the sentiment of the entire party in saying with the strongest emphasis that it makes all the difference in the world to be conducted through a strange city by a scholarly man like Mr. Wright or to go with the conventional guide. Some of his literary illustrations on historical points were delightful. For instance, in one place he read a charming extract from Elihu Burritt's "A Walk from London to Land's End," and in another a passage from one of Davenant's dramas, both of which were deliciously apropos. Our last excursion in Plymouth was an enjoyable trip to the beautiful Mount Edgcumbe Park, the estate of the Earl of Mount Edgcumbe, special permission having been obtained from his lordship by the Evangelical Free Church Council. The place is reached

The Pilgrims in Plymouth

Mayor Bond.

Mrs. Bond.

by means of a little steamer, and after a two hours' ramble in groves and gardens again we stood upon its deck and exchanged regretful farewells. One of the party in behalf of all thanked our English friends for their innumerable courtesies, all joined in singing, "Blest be the tie that binds," and after repeated hand-shakings we went our separate ways.

But the cream of the Plymouth visit was the reception in Guildhall on Friday evening by the mayor and mayoress, at which about three hundred of the leading citizens were present. The interior of this fine municipal building was superbly decorated for the occasion, potted plants, palms, draperies, intertwined flags of the two nations, and colored fairy lights being tastefully displayed. The rich blue carpet was thickly covered with a profusion of Oriental rugs

The Guildhall, Plymouth, as arranged for the Reception.

and skins, and on either side of the room were arcades divided off by large pillars into sitting rooms, screened in front with Japanese hangings. Outside the pillars were life-size figures representing the fine arts. Near the memorial window, which represents the departure of the Pilgrim Fathers, was a raised platform where the mayor, Alderman Bond, stood when he welcomed us most felicitously as "hostages of peace." Fitting replies were made by Rev. Messrs. Dunning, Dexter, Robinson, Soule, and Hon. J. A. Lane. The mayor wore his official robe, an imposing scarlet gown trimmed with black velvet and sable, and lined with white satin. Over this was a series of massive gold chains, from which depended the municipal seal. Ladies will be interested to know that black satin, Duchess lace, and diamonds formed the essential points of Mrs. Bond's dress, but her grace and urbanity far outshone the brilliancy of her jewels.

In order to appreciate the full significance of this function it should be remembered that the office of an English mayor is a purely honorable and not a salaried position, and carries far more distinction with it than a similar position in the average American city. Those who enjoyed his hospitality at the time of the International Council will have some conception of the privileges we experienced through his courtesy. The full band of the Welsh regiment, by kind permission of its colonel, furnished grand instrumental music, and the famous tenor from Exeter Cathedral, J. Dean Trotter, was among the soloists. Some of the American speakers followed our home custom of addressing the mayor as "Your Honor," which seemed to amuse our English friends, who restrict themselves to the simpler form of "Mr. Mayor." But never could the American title be more worthily bestowed than in the case of Mr. Bond, who is enthusiastically beloved by the citizens.

Let no one suppose, however, that *The Congregationalist's* Pilgrimage Party is having only a round of social gayeties. Beneath these enjoyable functions it is easy to see that Christian fellowship is the golden link which binds us together, and friends at home would be gratified, and perhaps astonished, to hear the applause whenever, in the public addresses, allusions are made to the impossibility of another war between the two great English-speaking races. It is worth crossing the ocean to see these evidences of international friendship.

"THE INTERESTING American visitors who appeared in our streets yesterday do not seem to be typical of Uncle Sam as he is depicted in the comic papers. Not one of them wore striped trousers or a star-spangled garment.

"The only goatee in the assembly belonged to an Englishman, and of 'guessing' and 'calculating' and boasting there was little or none. Some spoke with a rising inflection, which was not at all nasal. The complexions were American, but faces were full-fleshed, and bodily framework sturdy.

"The speeches, however, were the feature of the evening,—cheery, eloquent, incisive, and suggestive. The talking on occasions of this sort is often formal and complimentary, and nothing else. The addresses of the visitors from the States last night were of a different stamp, and it was an intellectual refreshment to listen to the vigorous and thoughtful utterances of men who, while modestly disclaiming any title to be reckoned as representative Americans, are certainly representative of some of the best elements of American society." — *A Plymouth Morning Paper.*

The Pilgrims in Exeter

IT is impossible to convey to the friends at home who are following our course with eager interest any idea of the reception accorded to us by English people. Ever since we landed in Plymouth it has been one continuous ovation. Our heads might be turned by this extraordinary attention did we not realize that it is offered to us, not as individuals, but as representatives of Puritan principles and ideas. We are only ciphers, and the significant figure is Congregationalism. We sometimes hear complaints at home of a lack of denominational loyalty, but the charge can never be made against any member of this party, for after visiting these sacred shrines and seeing how our polity is cherished by our brethren on this side of the Atlantic we realize anew what a price was paid for our religious liberty, and are proud of the glorious inheritance bequeathed to us.

Rev. W. J. Evans.

We reached Exeter about six P.M., via the London and Southwestern express, compartments in first-class carriages having been reserved for our use. A fraternal welcome was awaiting us at the station in the person of Rev. W. Justin Evans, pastor of the Southernhay Congregational Church, who escorted us to the Rougemont Hotel. On the landing of the principal staircase is a beautiful historical window to which, just then, we could give only a passing glance as the officials of the cathedral were waiting to conduct us through the building. The window illustrates the scene from Richard III, in which that ill-favored monarch exclaims to my Lord of Buckingham:—

> "Richmond! when last I was at Exeter,
> The Mayor, in courtesy, shewed me the castle,
> And called it *Rougemont*; at which name I started,
> Because a bard of Ireland told me once
> I should not live long after I saw *Richmond*."

It was an ideal time of day for one's first entrance into an English cathedral, just as the rays of a June sunset were stealing through the "storied windows richly dight," lighting up the "high embower'd roof," bringing into clear relief every detail of rich carving and intensifying the sense of grandeur by sending its golden shafts far down the Norman nave into remotest recess of aisle and choir. We

The Book of the Pilgrimage

The Cathedral Church, Exeter.

The Pilgrims in Exeter

assembled in the chapter house where Canon Atherton, representing the Dean and Chapter, received us cordially, saying that we are all working for the same great purpose, and in God's work we are linked across the ages as we are across the miles that separate us. Dr. Robie made a fitting response in behalf of the pilgrims, after which Canon Edmonds officiated as guide. In what he modestly termed an informal talk he gave us a choice lecture on mediæval art in his outline of the history and architecture of the stately edifice. We are realizing more and more what it is to have men like him act as interpreters and guides. The original Domesday Book of the five western counties which has been in the library since the tenth century, also the charter of Edward the Confessor, founding the cathedral, and the thirteenth century Psalter were among the articles of interest exhibited. The pulpit in memory of Coleridge Patteson, the queer little gal'ery where the minstrels played in olden times, and the bishop's throne, made without a nail in it, so that it could be taken

Canon Edmonds.

down and hidden away in times of danger, — which was actually done more than once, — were other objects explained with an elegance of diction and manner which charmed us all. To see Exeter Cathedral, under the direction of Canon Edmonds, was for the party a peculiarly fortunate introduction to English ecclesiastical architecture. In a marvelously simple manner the evolution of styles from the earliest Norman to the latest development of the Gothic was made beautifully clear, and at every point an illustration in stone was before our eyes, so skillfully did our leader conduct the party from point to point of his much-loved edifice, every stone of which he knows, every stone of which has a story, and he the infallible interpreter.

At this point, when both sense and imagination were held captive, a new delight was added by the sound of exquisite music from the organ (a remarkably fine instrument with a case of notable beauty), which stands midway down the nave, thus breaking its long perspective. The cathedral organist, Mr. D. J. Wood, held us entranced with the strains of Mendelssohn's Fourth Sonata, and other selections, until the gathering darkness warned us that we must return to the hotel. Unused to the long English twilights, we were astonished to find that it was now eight o'clock. We had not yet dined, and at nine we were due at Mr. Evans' church for a public reception! We deplored our late arrival, but our Noncon-

Canon Atherton.

formist friends, who had patiently waited for more than an hour, appreciated the unavoidable causes of delay and kindly condoned the seeming discourtesy.

When we entered the church, which was tastefully decorated for the occasion with flowers, British and American flags, and Y. P. S. C. E. emblems, the large congregation rose *en masse* and welcomed us with clapping of hands. The appropriate hymn, "We come unto our fathers' God," was then sung in a way that puts our best congregational singing at home entirely in the shade. Mr. Evans made a breezy address, in which he said that there was too much of Christ in the churches of both lands ever to allow them to fight one another. Their faith was one, their interests were common, and the victory of one was the success of the other. Equally fervent were the words of Rev. D. P. McPherson, on behalf of the Baptists, who claimed that some of the Pilgrim Fathers were undoubtedly of that denomination. The pastors of all the other dissenting churches in this Queen City of the west of England, also Mr. A. W. Tuckwell, representing the Young People's Societies of Christian Endeavor, alternated with half a dozen Americans in brief, pithy speeches in which every allusion to the strong tie which binds the two nations together elicited enthusiastic applause. One cannot resist the conviction that this little body of itinerant Congregationalists is being used, in the providence of God, to cement the bond by showing in miniature, as it were, the real feeling that exists between the English-speaking races.

It was nearly eleven o'clock when the exercises closed by the congregation singing lustily together, "The Son of God goes forth to war." Our considerate hosts accepted the validity of weariness on the part of the American clergymen as an excuse for not preaching the next day, although Rev. E. K. Holden, of Bridgeport, generously consented to occupy Mr. Evans' pulpit, and was listened to by a large congregation. Sunday was passed quietly in attendance upon divine service at the Nonconformist churches in the morning and the cathedral in the afternoon, some of us going later to the house of Mr. Henry Tolson, where we enjoyed our first glimpse of a typical English home.

When we recalled all that had transpired since landing only three days before, the writer was reminded of what Professor Henry Drummond said during his last visit to America. A great deal of enjoyment had been crowded into two particular days when he was the guest of a certain well-known Northampton gentleman. On his departure Professor Drummond exclaimed, "Is it possible that I've been here only forty-eight hours!" Then, stretching himself to his fullest height, he added, "Well, this is what expands and enriches life and makes it worth the living."

The Pilgrims in Wells and Glastonbury

WE felt the force of Madame de Staël's famous aphorism, that "traveling is the saddest of all pleasures," when we turned away from Devonshire with its sea-girt coast and wind-swept moors, its rugged cairns and giant tors, a region invested by Kingsley with immortal charm and endeared from henceforth to the New-World pilgrims as the place where they first experienced the boundless measure of English hospitality. The same generous welcome awaited us, however, at Wells, a quiet old town nestling in a pleasant valley at the foot of the Mendip Hills. Here, as elsewhere, Nonconformist friends were on hand to "greet the coming and speed the parting guest," our special *cicerone* being Rev. T. J. Kightley, pastor of the little Congregational church. He is a delightful old gentleman whose slender figure, silvery locks, and courtly manners reminded one strongly of Dr. C. A. Bartol of Boston.

Before conducting us through the cathedral he bade us linger on the widespreading lawn in order to feast our eyes upon the marvelously sculptured western façade of the cathedral and take in the full beauty of all its surroundings. What an impression of stillness and antiquity is given by the hoary edifice rising from its sea of greensward, its southern side overlooking a wealth of blooming gardens, and beyond them the old moat shadowed by mighty elms! Our strenuous American life seemed to gather an ineffable peace as we loitered without or followed our guide within, listening as he told us, with painstaking fidelity, the story of some valiant life enshrined in monument or effigy, or as he pointed out the different periods of architecture in traceried window and Gothic arch. We visited the chapter house, the only one in England that has two stories, going up the unique and beautiful staircase which branches on one side to the covered stone bridge leading to the Vicars' close, and on the other to the chapter house itself.

Rev. T. J. Kightley.

This is a fascinating room with deep window-jambs embellished with rows of ball-flower ornaments peculiar to the Decorated period, a place to hold an antiquarian spellbound.

From here we went to the Bishop's palace, which is ideally situated in the midst of luxuriant gardens and intrenched by the old moat on whose placid waters the white swans were floating like stately lilies. The figure of Bishop Ken seemed to

The Book of the Pilgrimage

emerge from the dim past and stroll again among the trees and flowers, or sit once more in his favorite nook on the wall above the moat, dulcimer in hand, singing his immortal hymns. Presently we were joined on the lawn by Bishop Kennion, a man of noble presence and spirit, who assured us that it was a pleasure to welcome us to a building so rich in history and so beautiful in situation. As we passed into the chapel it seemed the most natural thing in the world for him to suggest that we sing together three stanzas of Bishop Ken's familiar hymn,

> All praise to thee, my God, this night,
> For all the blessings of the light.

His own cultivated voice led the amateur chorus and also in our recital of the Lord's Prayer which followed. How simple and sincere and dignified it all seemed! And how it enhances the value of our Christian faith to pause in our journeying for these little spontaneous services of devotion! They make us feel that we are not merely conventional tourists but pilgrims indeed to "the city that hath foundations whose builder and maker is God." The bishop's benediction and the impression of his grace and urbanity are among the precious memories which we shall carry away with us from this ancient ecclesiastical city.

These rare privileges of the morning put us in just the right mood to enjoy a visit to Glastonbury in the afternoon. All the conditions of weather, scenery, companionship, and local tradition were perfectly adapted to awaken fancy as we drove in open carriages toward the "fair vale of Avalon," where, according to tradition, Joseph of Arimathea landed and built the first church in England, and where King Arthur and Guinevere lie buried. The pastor of the Congregational church, Rev. W. P. Hogben, and several other English friends, among them Mrs.

Bishop Kennion.

The Bishop's Palace, Wells.

The Pilgrims in Wells and Glastonbury

The Cathedral Church, Wells.

The Book of the Pilgrimage

Clark, a daughter of John Bright, were waiting to proffer the customary warm welcome. They joined us, too, in our walk to the old Abbey, enough of whose majestic ruins remains to give a correct idea of the extent of ground originally covered by the ancient pile.

In the shadow of these ruined fragments of a once glorious structure, and fresh from the almost perfect group of cathedral buildings at Wells, we remembered Canon Edmonds' suggestive remarks at Exeter in anticipation of this day's experiences, and we were impressed at the striking commentary time has supplied in the old truth, " He that findeth his life shall lose it, and he that loseth his life for my

St. Joseph's Chapel, Glastonbury Abbey.

sake shall find it." At Wells they builded a house to the glory of God and for the benefit of men, with no barriers between priest and people. At Glastonbury an all-powerful monastic order reared walls to keep out sin and the world, in order that those within the sacred precincts should forever be undisturbed in the selfish enjoyment of personal culture and private devotion ! The one temple is still a place for ministry to souls, the other is a mass of crumbling ruins.

Alderman J. G. L. Bulleid, president of the Antiquarian Society, summarized in graphic fashion the history of the Abbey from its foundation to its fall, and pointed out such of the remarkable architectural features as have resisted the slow touch of time. The mystic thorn tree, fabled to have been planted by Joseph of Arimathea,

The Pilgrims in Wells and Glastonbury

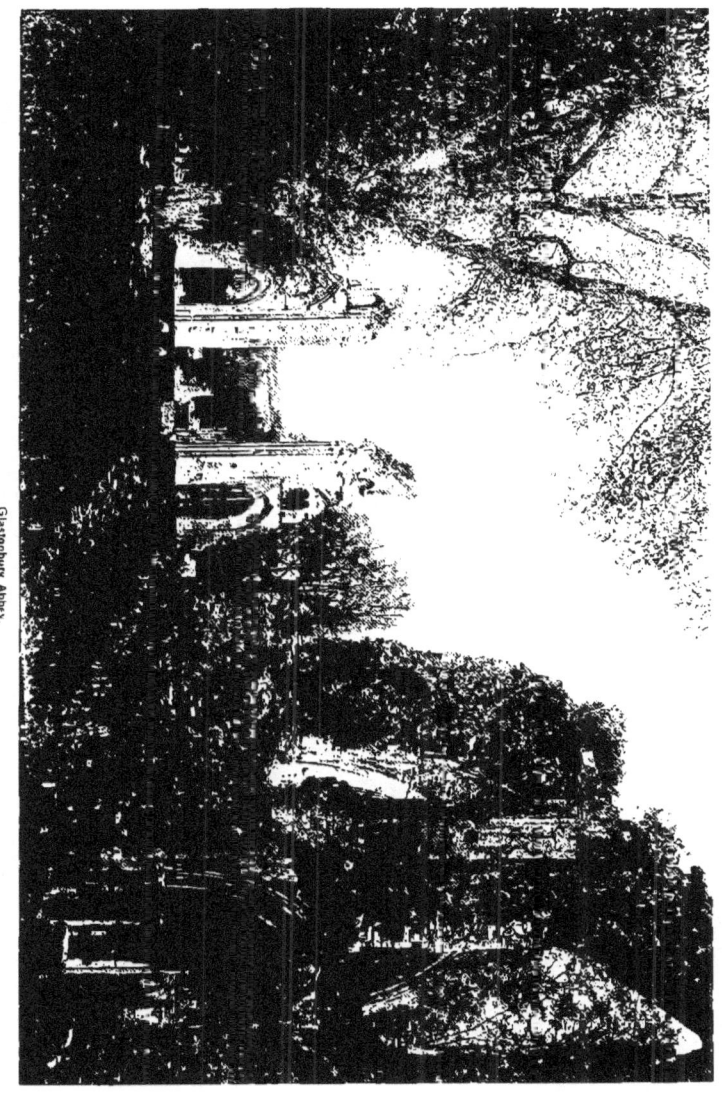

Glastonbury Abbey.

The Book of the Pilgrimage

The Pilgrims at Glastonbury, 15 June, 1896.

and whose offshoots still bear hawthorn blossoms in the midst of winter snows, rises against the wall.

Not far off is St. Michael's Tor, from which may be gained an entrancing view of the valley so beautifully described by Tennyson:—

> Deep-meadowed, happy, fair with orchard lawns,
> And bowery hollows, crowned with summer seas.

It was an hour to close one's eyes and dream. From the lofty turrets, overgrown with ivy, one could again hear the bell that "warned the cowled brother from his midnight cell." Through those massive arches again reverberated the *Tibi gloria, Domine*, of white-robed priests; down the mouldering aisles crept the wail of *Misereres*. The whole story of Arthur wove its spell about us as never before. Who says that he exists only in legend? Did not our eyes see him that summer afternoon, the very flower of British chivalry, riding with his stainless knights on to his glorious coronation in the church? Did we not see Guinevere robed for her bridal, coming forth on that glad May morning to meet the king, her hand in Arthur's but her heart with Lancelot? Did we not follow them through all the common tragedy that ensued, till penitence had wrought

Rev. W. P. Hogben.

its purifying work, and sin and failure were buried deep in the sea of forgiveness? We even saw in imagination the tower of Almesbury rising in the distance where for three years the repentant queen, as abbess, prayed and fasted and distributed dole to expiate her sin till she passed "to where beyond these voices there is peace." It was at Glastonbury that the Holy Grail was housed; it was here the stoled fathers met the bier bearing the form of Arthur when wounded to his death. To the solemn sound of chanted orison they lowered the body into the ground before the altar in St. Joseph's wattled church, and with his ashes mingle those of the golden-haired Guinevere. Only a romance? True; but one that holds in it the eternal verities of right and wrong, one that has had power for a thousand years to sway human hearts. Let critics dispute as they may whether the locality of the Arthurian legends be in the north or the south of Britain, for us they will ever be associated with the region whose fair expanse was spread before our vision on that June afternoon.

Enriching as the day had been thus far, one more pleasure awaited us in the form of a strawberry tea in the Sunday-school rooms of Mr. Hogben's church. There was no glamour of tradition, no æsthetic carving or coloring in the plain edifice, but there was the deeper satisfaction which arises from Christian fellowship. Nor were touches of beauty altogether lacking, for the small room was transformed into the semblance of a veritable garden by a profusion of flowers and ferns tastefully arranged. And how attractive the tables were with their heaped-up baskets of

The Book of the Pilgrimage

luscious strawberries and dainty edibles of various kinds! It was an unqualified joy to hold converse with these hospitable people who made us feel indeed that

> Kind hearts are more than coronets,
> And simple faith than Norman blood.

After doing ample justice to the viands provided for our bodily refreshment we adjourned to the main audience room for a brief season of song and prayer, led by Mr. Hogben. A letter was read from Rev. Mr. Rawlinson, president of the Somerset Congregational Union, regretting his unavoidable absence, and remarks were made by Messrs. N. W. Littlefield and W. F. Whittemore of the party. The meeting closed by singing, with uncommon fervor, "The church's one foundation." There was time for a short visit to the Museum before driving back to Wells in the light of a lovely sunset that flooded with roseate hue the entire landscape, from the turrets of the ruined Abbey to the roofs of humble cottages in the peaceful valley.

Before entering the hotel we indulged in one more ramble along the old moat, and then assembled at eight o'clock for a substantial dinner at the White Swan, a typical English inn, outwardly attractive, with window boxes of flowering plants, and inwardly comfortable to the last degree. The bedroom capacity of the house being unequal to the demands of our large party, some of us were privileged to lodge in the pretty cottages which border the cathedral lawn, and constitute one of the charming features of Wells. Before separating for the night we again joined in singing Bishop Ken's hymn, and for most of us was fulfilled at least one of its petitions— "Oh, may sweet sleep mine eyelids close!"

THEY were cordially received by His Lordship on the lawn, who, addressing them, said it gave him great pleasure to welcome them to that cathedral and that house so rich in history and so beautiful in its situation. He was glad and felt more and more thankful that the same good feeling existed among men of different thoughts, ways, and labors, and that they could appreciate one another's work and shake hands across the line which they might deem needful in defining their conception of their duty. This did not a little to broaden their fellowship and cheer them in their work. They might not see eye to eye in every respect, but they might be united heart to heart in closest sympathy. He held Dr. Dale, to whom reference had been made, as a personal friend and he respected his manly and sincere devotion to the principles he conscientiously held. English churchmen had benefited by the studies of Dr. Dale, whose writings were highly esteemed by them. Alluding to the title pilgrims, His Lordship remarked that they were all pilgrims and hoped to arrive at a common home. — *West of England Advertiser.*

The Pilgrims in Salisbury and Bemerton

WHAT has become of those "brief, light, pleasant rains" which the guidebooks affirm are peculiar to this climate? We supposed that an umbrella would be a *sine qua non* for each day's excursion, although John Burroughs declares that all one has to do in England to avoid a shower is to get over the hedge into the next lot. But thus far sunshine has smiled upon our pathway, and the Tuesday morning we started for Salisbury was no exception.

Special carriages were attached to the regular up-train, which reached the city at ten o'clock, and we were met at the station by several of the Free Church ministers and two of the city councilors. Both of the latter had recently visited "the States" and seemed glad to reciprocate the courtesies accorded them across the Atlantic. Carriages conducted us at once to the Congregational Church, and after a season of social intercourse we repaired to the adjoining lecture hall, where a sumptuous breakfast had been provided by Rev. E. Hassan and a few friends. This is the first of those "semi-gustatory, semi-oratorical receptions" of which Dr. Clark prophesied that we should have our fill; and if this

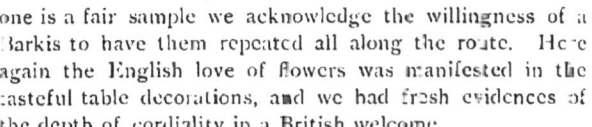

Rev. Edward Hassan.

one is a fair sample we acknowledge the willingness of a Barkis to have them repeated all along the route. Here again the English love of flowers was manifested in the tasteful table decorations, and we had fresh evidences of the depth of cordiality in a British welcome.

The ex-mayor, Mr. E. F. Pye-Smith, presided, and paid a delicate tribute to American literature by embellishing his graceful address with copious quotations from our own poets. His opening sentence reflects the spirit of all that was said on this delightful occasion. "We can boast no autocrat at this breakfast-table to speak to you kindly words of wisdom, but in humbler manner I desire, on behalf of the Nonconformists of the city, to give you a very hearty welcome and to wish you God-speed on your journey as you

E. F. Pye-Smith, Esq.

The Book of the Pilgrimage

The Cathedral Church, Salisbury

The Pilgrims in Salisbury and Bemerton

> ' Trace back
> The hero-freighted Mayflower's prophet track
> To Europe.'"

The same ring of friendly appreciation sounded through the address that followed from Mr. Hassan. No wonder that our hearts were touched and that reciprocally warm sentiments were evoked from the three pilgrims who responded, namely, Dr. Dunning, Mr. Leete, and Dr. Robinson.

It would have been a pleasure to spend the entire day in such a congenial atmosphere, but our hosts realized that the sub-dean, Dr. Bourne, was awaiting us at the cathedral and they kindly escorted us thither. All the architectural features of this noble pile, which Goldwin Smith calls "the most perfect monument of mediæval Christianity in England," were carefully explained by Dr. Bourne as he stood in the west front doorway. Here and at Wells are the two best specimens of the cathedral close, and we saw both under conditions that will never be forgotten. But the glory of Salisbury, its lofty, slender spire, was encased in a scaffolding for repairs and therefore viewed at a disadvantage. Our time being limited, we were obliged to decline an invitation from the bishop to go over the palace, but we took a short stroll in the lovely deanery gardens where Dean Boyle, a man of most affable manners, received us under the shade of a wide-spreading tree. He chatted familiarly of American matters and spoke affectionately of the late Dr. Dale, whose acquaintance he enjoyed for many years and to whom he alludes in his "Recollections," a book quite recently published.

Dean Boyle.

Sub-Dean Bourne.

It seemed a natural transition from this tranquil spot to the little church in Bemerton, where the saintly George Herbert ministered for less than two years, but left a memory that has been kept fragrant for more than two centuries. The parish churches of England, no less than the stately cathedrals, always appeal to the Christian heart, and there is no sweeter music in the world than their mellow chimes pealing

> O'er earth's green fields and ocean's wave-beat shore.

This tiny edifice, the smallest of its kind with one exception in England, was also undergoing repairs and did not present its best appearance. But the workmen suspended operations while we grouped ourselves near the chancel and listened to

The Book of the Pilgrimage

BEMERTON — The Church — The Rectory.

The Pilgrims in Salisbury and Bemerton

Mr. Whittemore as he read a portion of Herbert's quaint poem on Sunday and also some familiar verses from "The Elixir," beginning with:—

> Teach me, my God and King,
> In all things thee to see,
> And what I do in anything
> To do it as for thee.

We were then led in prayer by Dr. Robie, the modest and scholarly New England parson who, in spirit and purpose, bears a strong resemblance to the unpretentious rector of long ago.

After this service, impressive both for its spontaneity and its suggestiveness, we crossed the street to the rectory and were cordially welcomed by Miss Warre, her brother, the canon, being unavoidably absent. Upon a tablet in the wall outside are inscribed these lines, which were written on the mouth of the chimney in the hall in Herbert's day:—

> TO MY SUCCESSOR.
>
> If thou chance to find
> A new house to thy mind,
> And built without thy cost,
> Be good to the poor,
> As God gave thee store,
> And then my labour's not lost.

The diminutive study remains just as he used it, and the old hall has been restored by the present rector. As we wandered from room to room and then passed through the drawing-room window into the peaceful rectory gardens beyond, wherein stands the medlar tree which tradition says was planted by this parish priest and poet, the place seemed filled with his presence. Day by day, during his brief but wonderful incumbency, he gathered the people from their tasks for worship, and the same bell, one of the uncommon kind known as Alphabet bells, that called plowman and servant to the house of God, still hangs in the small bell tower. This is claimed to be the first great historical instance of the English country clergyman impressing upon his parishioners the duty of daily devotions in the church.

There was time before taking the train for Winchester to inspect the massive earth mounds, now called Old Sarum, on a neighboring hill, and some of the party took the opportunity to drive across the lonely expanse of Salisbury Plain to Stonehenge. In both places these monuments of the wild tribal wars of the ancient Britons, telling of days of bloody superstition and blind submission to priestly power, offered a sharp contrast to the scene of spiritual calm that we had just left. The sacrificial fires of heathen rites no longer blaze on these quiet hilltops, for now over the whole land reigns the Prince of Peace, whose service is perfect freedom.

The Pilgrims in Winchester and Farnham

LATE in the afternoon we reached Winchester and were met at the station, with a cordiality which has ceased to surprise, but never fails to charm us, by Mayor Dyer, Rev. C. E. Dickinson, and two other gentlemen. We were driven directly to the cathedral, where Canon Warburton stood at the great west door ready to conduct us through the majestic edifice. This is the largest of the English minsters, and around it clusters a wealth of historic interest scarcely paralleled elsewhere. It seemed an utterly hopeless task, in the brief hour at our command, to take even a cursory glance at the interior, much less to inspect anything in detail. If left to ourselves, we should probably have wandered around in aimless fashion, oppressed with a sense of the difficulty of trying to do anything in so short a time. But through the courtesy of Dean Stephens and under the leadership of our accomplished guide, who possessed the art of taking salient features, either historic or architectural, and presenting them

Rev. C. E. Dickinson.

clearly yet concisely, we made a reasonably satisfactory tour through the huge building. It was one of the places, however, where the inadequacy of time was deeply felt. But several of the party are not altogether novices in travel on English soil, and their knowledge is often helpfully imparted as we talk over our Pilgrimage *en route*.

On this occasion what we lost in actual vision was partially made up by the livelier play of imagination prompted by the sunset hour. In proportion as the light waned, figures from the dim and distant past took on a bolder outline. Far in the background stood Alfred, patron of art and letters, compiler of the first Domesday Book, and founder of that group of monastic buildings whose site alone now suggests his tranquil reign of eighteen years. Then came an imposing procession of sovereigns, for Winchester, it should be remembered, was for a long time the English capital. In the time of Henry I it rivaled London in splendor and renown, but

The Mayor of Winchester.

gradually declined in importance, though still eloquent with a thousand noble memories. As we paused for a moment at the tombs and chantries of this royal retinue the magic wand of the canon's words touched into lifelike reality each character and period. Not kings alone but eminent bishops passed in review, chief among them William of Wykeham, whose bold conceit of grafting the Perpendicular upon the Norman style of architecture is everywhere in evidence, especially in the long, beautiful nave, one of the finest specimens of Perpendicular extant. We were reminded, too, that he was the "father of the English public school system," and gave an impulse to education such as the world had never seen. Of the three great schools which play in the famous cricket matches — Eton, Harrow, and Winchester — the last has the prestige of excelling in antiquity, having existed for five hundred years.

Dean Stephens.

Another of the statesmen bishops of that period, Henry Beaufort, lies in effigy in a stately chantry, the strong face looking selfish and avaricious even in stone. When we passed, later on, through the deanery gardens we saw the spot where Bishop Ken, afterwards of Bath and Wells, bravely took his stand against Nell Gwynne, thus defying the displeasure of the "Merry Monarch," who, after all, respected the bishop's courage. The quaint old chair in which Queen Mary sat when she came to the city "in a cruel wind and violent downpour of rain" recalled the fact that it was Bishop Gardiner who officiated at her ill-starred marriage to Philip of Spain. Standing by this chair came a thought, hardly in chronological sequence, of Sir Walter Raleigh, and an impression, since verified, that in Winchester he wrote the beautiful poem beginning : —

> Give me my scallop shell of quiet,
> My staff of faith to walk upon,
> My scrip of joy, immortal diet,
> My bottle of salvation,
> My gown of glory (hope's true gage!),
> And thus I'll take my Pilgrimage.

Possibly the cruel scenes of Mary's reign suggested Raleigh's imprisonment in the Tower. But more likely the association of ideas arose from a vision of Cromwell's troops ruthlessly despoiling the treasures of the cathedral as they marched noisily down the splendid nave, shattering peerless stained glass and hacking noble sculptures. Another sharp mental contrast was offered by seeing on the floor in Prior Silkstede's chapel, covered with a dingy mat, a slab to the memory of the gentle angler, Sir Izaak Walton. What incongruity between the iconoclasm of the Roundheads and the serenity of the old man taking his ease upon the banks of the Itchen, which still gurgles through the green gardens! Twilight shadows were

The Book of the Pilgrimage

The Cathedral Church, Winchester.

The Pilgrims in Winchester and Farnham

fast enfolding us, and the size of the huge gray pile, overrun here and there with ivy, seemed intensified in the somber light, while the ponderous central tower seemed more than ever depressed under the weight of centuries and darkness.

Refreshed by dinner at the excellent George Hotel, we wended our way to British Hall, where the Nonconformists of Winchester had assembled in large numbers to greet our party. Passing through a corridor lined with palms and potted plants, we emerged into a large, handsomely appointed room, decorated with choice flowers and banners of the two nations harmoniously blended. Councilor Goodbody, one of the four who met us at the station, had thoughtfully had placed upon the walls a fine engraving of the landing of the Pilgrim Fathers in America. The mayor and mayoress, with pastors of the various Independent churches, acted in the capacity of host, and the spirit of genuine friendliness manifested by all was enough to warm the cockles of the coldest heart. The time spent in the cathedral seemed all too brief, but our regret was even greater that we had such a limited opportunity for converse with this body of fellow-Christians who outvied each other in hospitality. They entertained us with music, speeches in which Rev. Morton Dexter and Rev. L. L. Wirt participated, and with toothsome refreshments, after which we adjourned to the chapel to enjoy two solos from the "Messiah," admirably rendered by Mr. Munden. The evening's pleasure, much of which was due to the forethought of Mr. E. Couzens, secretary of the local committee, was brought to a close by the congregation singing "All hail the power of Jesus' name."

It was a weary set of pilgrims who sought their couches about midnight, but notwithstanding they were on hand on the morning of June 17 for such a unique celebration of Bunker Hill Day as never fell to the lot of Americans before. The whirligig of time brings about strange changes, and it was a curious coincidence that on the anniversary of that memorable battle between British and Americans we should have been entertained at Farnham Castle by the lord bishop of Winchester, Dr. Randall Davidson, and his amiable wife, who is a daughter of the late Archbishop Tait.

Until the English language has a richer vocabulary than now no words can do justice to the occasion. Of all the bishops' houses in the land no other is more grandly situated, and no other castle, not even Windsor, has been held so long by an unbroken succession of men. It stands on an eminence overlooking the valley of the Wye, famous for its hop gardens, and to the east is the great deer park, covering over 300 acres, the only episcopal deer park remaining in England in which there is historical evidence that deer have been kept for 600 years. His Lordship and wife graciously received us at the very entrance, and we assembled immediately on the spacious staircase, with its magnificent oak carvings, passing along the way traversed by kings and bishops for a thousand years, as the bishopric of Winchester dates from the days of Ethelbald.

In this place of inspiring memories, standing midway on the stairs, His Lordship gave us a wonderfully interesting lecture, outlining the stirring events of this early

The Book of the Pilgrimage

The Entrance.　　　FARNHAM CASTLE　　　The Keep Garden.
Castle as seen from the park.

The Pilgrims in Winchester and Farnham

period, down through the days of Henry de Blois, who made the castle a formidable fortress, through the miserable reign of John, of whom the chronicler said, "Hell was made fouler by the entrance of his soul," on to the Tudor period, mentioning the names of Fox, Wolsey, Gardiner, Mary Tudor, and hosts of others who had passed in panorama before us only the preceding night. He depicted the period of the civil wars, when the castle was tossed like a shuttlecock between the contending armies, and came at length to modern days when the preceding incumbent, Bishop Thorold, undertook "to make it as easy as possible for a successor to reside at the castle" by adding modern improvements. Here the unhappy Mary stopped on her way to Winchester to marry Philip of Spain, here Elizabeth frequently tarried, and James I made himself so obnoxious by his costly visits that the bishop tartly inquired "if he looked on Farnham as an inn."

This remarkably lucid historical sketch, occupying about an hour, was the best preparation possible for our subsequent inspection of the castle and its old keep, which is approached through a subterranean passage. We were divided into four groups, one each under the guidance of His Lordship, Mrs. Davidson, and two other members of the household. Among the points of special interest was the bedchamber of Bishop Morley, chaplain to Charles II, in his exile, and practically the rebuilder

Bishop Davidson.

of the castle. It is a bare little room, for he was a man of ascetic habits, who rose at 5 A.M. the year round, took only one full meal a day, and denied himself the comfort of a fire in the coldest weather. A single small window faced the east and a dark recess served as a "penitential cell." Other fascinating places were the old thirteenth century kitchen, probably the work of De Lucy, with its immense fireplace at one end, and the stately banquet hall where half the sovereigns of England have sat at meat. A balustraded gallery runs round two sides, and over the richly carved fireplace hangs the melancholy portrait of Bishop

Mrs. Davidson.

Morley. On the lintel of one huge beam is inscribed the old French motto, *Au Dieu foy; aux amis foyer* (To God faith; to friends the hearth).

It was in this room, teeming with historic associations, that we were entertained at luncheon, after a most uplifting service in the domestic chapel at which Mr. Davidson wore the blue ribbon and seal of the Garter over his bishop's robe. The former he kept on during the meal. The chapel is a long, narrow room separated from the corridor (where stands the organ which Mrs. Davidson played) by a beautiful Renaissance screen of openwork. The stalled seats, which our little company

The Book of the Pilgrimage

nearly filled, are of rich dark wood and the wall panels are carved with designs of cherubs' heads, fruit, and flowers. The opening hymn,

O God, our help in ages past,

the Scripture lesson and prayers drew us all nearer to the throne of heavenly grace and deepened in each soul a sense of the preciousness of our common Christian faith. One of the most enriching experiences of our trip thus far was this chapel service, together with the opportunity of breaking bread with a host and hostess like Bishop and Mrs. Davidson, whose urbanity and generous hospitality will never be forgotten by *The Congregationalist's* pilgrims. The tenor of his formal greeting, given at the close of the meal, may be inferred from these characteristic sentences: "In our political, our social, our civic life, no less than in our religious life, mutual toleration and friendship and affection will bring peace instead of strife. . . . We shall be thankful indeed if, even in the smallest degree, such a gathering as ours to-day tends to render absolutely impossible what would undoubtedly be the greatest disaster the world has ever seen. I thank you for coming here to-day. I thank you for the kind way you have received what little my wife and I have tried to do in welcoming you, not to a private home, but rather to a great historic house which we are privileged for the time to hold in trust for the good of all."

Dr. Guinness Rogers was kindly included among the guests, and he, with Dr. Dunning and Hon. J. A. Lane, made fitting responses. As we drove away from the castle in a gentle rain, our hearts filled with deepest gratitude for the privileges of the morning, we carried with us memories as fragrant as the flowers which bloomed in every room and added the sweetness of their welcome to the words spoken by the noble bishop and his wife.

On our return to Winchester there was time for a brief visit to the Holy Cross Hospital, an ancient almshouse built by Henry of Blois in 1136, and designed originally for the support of "thirteen poor men, feeble, and so reduced in strength that they cannot support themselves." Thirteen of the poorest boys from St. Swithin's School were also sent there for a daily portion of food, and here the "wayfarer's dole" is still dispensed. The dole is a relic of the old custom of offering food to all chance comers and in deference to lang syne we took our bit of bread and a sip of rather attenuated beer. In the fifteenth century the establishment received the high-sounding name of the Almshouse of Noble Poverty from Cardinal Beaufort, who endowed it liberally, providing for an increase in the number of beneficiaries, and the annual income from the two foundations is now about £3,500. This is quite munificent for the modest needs of the few venerable brethren who live in the row of little stone cottages facing the quadrangle, and who look picturesque enough as they walk across the green, or among the flowers in the tiny gardens, clad in long black or plum-colored gowns, with a silver cross hung over the breast. The number of residents is strictly limited by the provisions of the two foundations, and they are chosen from the class that has "seen better days." The early grant also stipulated that

The Pilgrims in Winchester and Farnham

St. Cross, Winchester.

By courtesy of The Churchman.

The Book of the Pilgrimage

dinners should be given each day to a hundred poor men, although this clause has long been a dead letter. But the room where they were accustomed to assemble, with smoke-begrimed roof, huge fireplace, and minstrel gallery, is still one of the notable features of the establishment. The group of buildings is most interesting and valuable from an architectural point of view, particularly the church, which is very fine Norman and has recently been restored and redecorated according to the ancient scheme of color discovered some years since by one of the brothers, himself

An old Engraving of "The Trusty Servant"

a mason. With his own feeble hands he toiled for several years almost alone, until the results of his labors, revealing the fine old walls, kindled the enthusiasm and secured the support of antiquarians and art lovers, who subscribed the necessary funds for a complete restoration. On our return from St. Cross we caught a glimpse of Winchester School, its glorious chapel and the quaint old picture of "The Trusty Servant" in the kitchen corridor, both commanding the interest of the pilgrims.

Surrounded by these associations of a past extending far back into the twelfth

The Pilgrims in Winchester and Farnham

century, the events of Bunker Hill Day seemed but of yesterday, and the clashing of political parties at home in connection with the Presidential conventions sounded discordant indeed in this place of tranquil beauty.

THE BISHOP'S SPEECH at the luncheon table was so charmingly expressed and breathed such a fine spirit that alike those who heard it and those who did not will be glad of the opportunity of reading it in full: "I am glad you have given us the very real and genuine pleasure of being our guests to-day. Few things would at any time give to me and to my wife greater satisfaction than to welcome those from across the Atlantic who have so many common associations with ourselves in the storied centuries that are gone. And when the visit has so peculiar a significance, bearing alike on the history of the past and on the possibilities of the future as has this visit of yours to England, the pleasure is made tenfold greater to us all. There are many points on which we differ. We don't necessarily bury our differences when we bury our strifes. The two things are quite distinct. The bitter and even savage strifes of two hundred and eighty years ago are, thank God, dead and buried to-day. Differences will no doubt continue to exist as long as men of different character, temperament, and sympathies try honestly to approach great subjects in the way in which God enables each to see them. I will not say that those differences are necessarily permanent, but we see no immediate prospect of their disappearance. Many think — I do not say they are wrong — that the variety of aspects in which the great truths of our common faith can be presented is in itself a gain. Unity and uniformity are two very different things, and, for myself, I should be sorry to see a dull uniformity take the place of the deep and stable unity which underlies so many surface differences. Along with you, I welcome Dr. Guinness Rogers as a representative, if I may so express it, of the sturdy side of our English Nonconformity. It is not my fault that there are not others with him here. I asked Dr. Mackennal, Dr. Horton, and Dr. Barrett, and I am exceedingly sorry that it was not possible for them to accept the invitation. We must all have been glad to learn from Dr. Guinness Rogers that his visit has, so far, done him no harm (laughter), and that he will go hence as sturdy as when he came. You represent, ladies and gentlemen, one of the elements in our national history. We in the Church of England value the manifold traditions which come down to us from former centuries. It is the union of many streams from many channels which makes our strength, and the traditions of Puritanism have for us their distinctive value not less than the traditions that come down in other ways (applause).

Our Puritan ancestors have as true a place in our history on this side the Atlantic as they have in yours on the other. To those who come across the sea to revisit their own old homes — for they are their own old homes — we in England will ever accord a ready and fraternal welcome. The circumstances are indeed different since Bishop Lancelot Andrewes sat in this hall while the Mayflower was crossing the Atlantic, and I venture to think there are some great truths better understood and appreciated now than they were in 1620. That particular epoch in our history will not repeat itself. We thank God and take courage as we reflect how in days to come that special care for truth as God has taught it to the individual soul, which has sometimes sundered men, seems likely to unite them closer and closer in reverence for the great verities we all hold in common. In our political, our social, our civic life, no less than in our religious life, mutual toleration and friendship and affection will bring peace instead of strife. Not one of us but looked with horror on the clouds that hovered overhead not many months ago. We shall be thankful, indeed if, even in the smallest degree, such a gathering as ours to-day tends to render absolutely impossible what would undoubtedly be the greatest disaster the world has ever seen. I thank you for coming here to-day. I thank you for the kind way you have received what little my wife and I have tried to do in welcoming you, not to a private home, but rather to a great historic house which we are privileged for the time to hold in trust for the good of all. I pray that the blessing of God may rest upon you when you return, and that the reminiscence of to-day, which will certainly be cherished most closely by us, may be among not the least inspiring of those which you will carry with you on your homeward way." — *The Christian Commonwealth.*

DR. GUINNESS ROGERS, in the course of his remarks at the bishop's luncheon, said: —

"On us rests a very solemn responsibility. We are the representatives of Christianity to a certain extent on both sides of the Atlantic, and on us rests very much of the responsibility of taking care that no false and foolish pride, no silly notions of diplomatic disputes, shall ever be allowed to come in and separate those who by every tie that nature can create and that God can give are inseparably bound." -- *The Christian Commonwealth.*

The Pilgrims in Oxford and Cambridge

IT is nothing uncommon for Americans to visit the two ancient seats of learning which are among the greatest glories of Great Britain, to view their gray, weather-stained edifices wrought with quaint, Gothic ornament, and to wander through their cloistered walks or over their grassy quadrangles. But it is most extraordinary when the fellows and masters of these institutions proffer their services as guides and give hours of their valuable time to the entertainment of strangers from the New World. Both at Oxford and Cambridge, however, this unusual privilege was enjoyed by *The Congregationalist's* Pilgrimage Party, and the academic cap and gown of our leader everywhere proved an open sesame to places not usually open to tourists. At Oxford we were thus conducted by Mr. Hall, whose affable manners and wise guidance made the hours spent in his society a pleasure never to be forgotten.

The apt saying of some one that the city is "bitterly historical" was brought forcibly to mind on finding that the large and handsome hotel to which we were assigned, The Randolph, was in close proximity to the Martyrs' Monument. This fine Gothic structure, which commemorates the burning at the stake of Latimer, Ridley, and Cranmer, stands in St. Giles, that long, continuous street having four names, but the exact spot of the martyrdom is designated by a cross in the pavement in front of Balliol. We did not undertake to "do" the twenty-one colleges, but by selecting six of the most typical we formed some ideas of the wealth of learning represented in this "metropolis of the muses."

Martyrs' Monument, Oxford.

Among those visited were ancient Merton, founded in 1264; Magdalen, memorable for its magnificent tower and the long, leafy avenue known as Addison's Walk; and Christ Church, back of which lie the lovely meadows, the pride of Oxford and the delight of all tourists. This last college was founded by Cardinal Wolsey, and in the old dining hall, with its wonderfully carved oak roof, is a bewildering array of portraits of statesmen, scholars, and poets; one of Henry VIII, by Holbein, is sure to attract notice; also the interesting faces of Ben Jonson, Sir Philip Sidney, Sir Robert Peel, and Hon. W. E. Gladstone.

The Pilgrims in Oxford and Cambridge

A striking external feature in all English colleges is the box of flowering plants placed outside the windows, making a glowing mass of bloom against the background of dingy stone walls. The founder of this pretty fashion of window gardening, John Kyrle, is honored with a portrait in Balliol, in the same room with Wickliffe, Browning, Tait, Manning, and a host of other eminent men. The Sheldonian Theater is where the degrees are conferred, and as we passed the grotesque stone busts on pedestals outside we recalled the racy letter that Phillips Brooks once wrote to

Principal Fairbairn.

his little niece, "Toodie," describing the ceremony when the honor was bestowed upon him. "My Doctor's gown," he wrote, "was red with black sleeves and is awfully pretty. It was only hired for the occasion, for it costs ever so much money and I did not care to buy one. So you will never see how splendid I looked in it, for I shall never have it on again."

Lowell, Holmes, and this season Ambassador Bayard are other Americans who have been similarly honored with degrees here. Near by is the famous Bodleian Library, a perfect treasure house of priceless manuscripts and autographs, illuminated missals and historic relics, not to mention its 300,000 books, representing every known de-

Mansfield College, Oxford.

The Book of the Pilgrimage

partment of literature. Another feature, different from anything we have at home, is the number of college chapels, often structures of great architectural beauty, with richly decorated windows and full of history and legend.

Interior of the Chapel, Mansfield College, Oxford

For our party, however, the crowning event at Oxford was the luncheon at Mansfield College. It is a great victory for Nonconformity that its theological school now has a home in this scholar's paradise, and that a man like Dr. Fairbairn, whose attainments and character have won universal respect, is the principal. The

The Pilgrims in Oxford and Cambridge

series of Puritan portraits in the dining hall furnished him a text for a fine post-prandial speech, in which he uttered this noble sentiment: "Nothing implies such a lack of faith as persecution, and nothing shows so large a faith as liberty."

Again in Cambridge, through the kind intervention of A. W. W. Dale, we enjoyed the exceptional advantage of having either a master or fellow to do the honors, Drs. Peele and Morgan serving us in the morning and Dr. Butler, master of Trinity, in the afternoon. An agreeable pause in the sight-seeing was afforded by a superb organ recital in one of the chapels by a nephew of Professor R. G. Moulton, of university extension fame. Immanuel College, so closely identified with the earliest pilgrim history, was of course visited. As Trinity holds a unique place in the group of seventeen colleges, being the largest and the one which entertains royalty when visiting Cambridge, a somewhat detailed account of our visit there may be of interest.

Dr. P. T. Forsyth

The office of master, corresponding to that of college president in America, is now filled by Henry Montagu Butler, D.D. He was cradled in an atmosphere of learning, his father having been Master of Harrow and afterwards Dean of Peterborough. The son has been the recipient of signal honor as a preacher, holding, among other offices, that of chaplain to the Queen, prebendary of St. Paul's, and examining chaplain to Archbishop Tait and the present primate of all England, Edward White Benson. Dr. Butler is a man of charming personality, who possesses the rare gift of making persons and events of the past throb with the life of to-day. Under the spell of his choice diction the old portraits on the walls seemed to step out of their frames and join our procession through rooms where the feet of kings, judges, bishops, and teachers had trod before us. There is a bit of romance, too, in his second marriage to which we could not be insensible, especially when

A. W. W. Dale, M. A.

Dr. Forsyth's Church.

The Book of the Pilgrimage

Immanuel College, Cambridge.

he wove into his fascinating web of talk anecdotes of "little Jim," his son of six, whose toy trumpet we noticed lying carelessly upon a table in one of the stately apartments in close proximity to objects of priceless value. When considerably beyond middle life Dr. Butler married Miss Ramsay, the Girton graduate of twenty, who carried off the prizes in Greek a few years ago, and the music of three little children's voices now resounds through the oaken-paneled rooms of old Trinity. Not long ago when Ambassador Bayard was a guest in the home, little Jim inquired: "Papa, what is an ambassador?" To which his father gave the wise reply: "An ambassador, my son, is a kind, good man who tries to make all good men friends with each other." Whereupon the child solemnly inquired: "Is he black?"

No words can describe the impressions which crowded upon us as we sat in the large, nobly proportioned drawing-room, Dr. Park occupying the Queen's chair, and listened to our genial host's account of bygone scenes which had transpired there. Looking through the diamond-shaped panes of the great bow window, across a little bit of a court, we saw where four typical men, Newton, Macaulay, Thackeray, and Lightfoot, once had their quarters. On the walls of this same grand apartment was

The Cam, Cambridge.

The Pilgrims in Oxford and Cambridge

Cambridge.

The Book of the Pilgrimage

a portrait of Elizabeth in the stiffest of brocades and the widest of ruffs, and another of Henry VIII, whom a student at one of the women's colleges wittily characterized as "the greatest widower of his age." This last painting was by a pupil of Holbein, and on grand occasions a reflector lamp is placed in front to show off the fine coloring. Here, too, was a portrait of the great Newton at nearly seventy, and bearing a striking resemblance to the late Dean Stanley, also several

The Great Court, Trinity College, Cambridge.

portraits of eminent masters and chancellors of the university, the latter always being a person of royal blood or a nobleman of high rank. The present incumbent is the Duke of Devonshire. Into this room Elizabeth once came with Lord Burleigh, and every sovereign since Anne's time has graced the apartment. Victoria came in state in 1847, when the prince consort was made chancellor, and again in her jubilee year. We were shown the state bedrooms, in which the appointments were far less elegant than in many an American home, but oh, what a wealth of portraits on the wall! A tender interest invested the picture of the Duke of Clarence, who occupied the room the night before receiving his LL.D. Shortly afterwards he died, and his father, the Prince of Wales, who took his M.A. at Cambridge, presented the son's portrait to Trinity.

Dr. H. M. Butler.

Other interesting rooms were those assigned to the judges when they come up to the assizes and practically take possession of the establishment. Dr. Butler facetiously remarked that the whole British constitution would probably come to an end if he, in his own house, should presume to act as host on these august occasions! They have a special kitchen and scullery set apart for their use, lest, as our host jokingly suggested, they be poisoned with ordinary food. Here, likewise, were faces of men who seemed like old friends when introduced in Dr. Butler's inimitable fashion,

The Pilgrims in Oxford and Cambridge

One of Lord Lyndhurst, son of the American painter, Copley, had a sad, sweet expression, and one of Justice Patteson, father of Coleridge Patteson, of missionary fame, was singularly attractive, one hand being placed behind his ear in the attitude of listening. An autograph letter accompanies the picture, in which the father speaks pathetically of "dear Coley" taking orders and going to far-off Melanesia, and the possibility of their never meeting again, a predict on only too soon verified.

Among the more vivid recollections which we shall retain of that enriching half day is the picture of Tennyson in his scarlet gown, the graceful, almost feminine head of Arthur Hallam, faces of illustrious statesmen of to-day — Balfour, Harcourt, and Speaker Gully — Bishop Wordsworth, a brother of the poet, in scarlet gown and white tippet, Whewell and Barrow, each of whom had an amazing range of knowledge, Westcott and Lightfoot placed side by side on the great oaken stairway, and the tall old clock on the stairs bequeathed by Sir Isaac Newton to Bentley, one of the most popular masters of Trinity. Then the walk in the lovely garden, where is reputed to be the finest bit of green in all England, a great emerald parallelogram which, in the language of tradition, "we rolls and we mows for a thousand years," and which Wordsworth's room overlooked — where is the artist in words to depict the witchery of the scene? In another garden we saw the lofty, spreading tree that nobody could name until Asa Gray came as a guest to Trinity and classified it as an ailanthus; and in the library the noble bust of Byron holding a copy of "Childe Harold" in the left hand, together with the original draft of Milton's "Paradise Lost" and an endless collection of other treasures, literary and scientific, that would require weeks to see satisfactorily.

From beginning to end the stay of the American pilgrims at Cambridge was a continual feast. Our headquarters were at the Bull, a quiet, well-kept inn, having a certain dignity consonant with its academic surroundings. Like the college buildings its gray façade was abloom with flowering plants. Our arrival was toward the close of a perfect June day, and we were driven at once to Edenfield, the beautiful home of Mr. and Mrs. Munsey, who had invited a large number of guests to meet us at a garden party. There were no formal speeches, but words of welcome from Rev. P. T. Forsyth, D.D., Mr. Dale, and others, and opportunity for social converse under the green trees, where the fragrance of exquisite roses was mingled with the aroma of tea and strawberries. Several of the same kind friends came to the station on our departure, and once more we fared forth laden with a deep sense of the blessedness of that Christian fellowship which has illumined all our way.

The Pilgrims in Bedford

A FAIRER June morning never dawned than the one when "the Pilgrim Fathers," as our party is now popularly called, turned their faces toward the shrine of Bunyan in the town of Bedford. We were met at the station by Mr. Greatheart in the person of Dr. John Brown, author of the delightful new Life of the tinker preacher, and a few other friends, who accompanied us first to the little village of Elstow, on the outskirts of Bedford, where Bunyan was born in 1628.

We halted at the quaint cottage by the roadside, and passed through the tiny hall to a diminutive garden in the rear. A room on the left, as we entered, was filled with souvenirs which a pleasant voiced woman offered for sale, and a little girl's face was pressed close against the latticed windows, filled with wondering awe at the sight of these strange Americans. This, then, was the place to which the immortal dreamer brought his young bride, "Not having so much household stuff as a dish or spoon betwixt us both." But she brought him, nevertheless, a precious dowry in the shape of "saintly memories of a godly home and trained instincts for

Dr. John Brown

good." And "she would beguile their summer evening walks and their fireside winter talks by memories of the good man, her father, who had gone to heaven." Thus were set in motion, in this humble cottage with rooms scarcely the size of the Columbia's staterooms, those influences which converted the "ungodliest fellow for swearing" in all the region round about into a preacher of world-wide renown.

Not far off is the village green where Bunyan was play-

Bunyan Meeting, Bedford.

The New World Pilgrims with Dr. John Br[...]

t the Old Moot Hall, Elstow, 19 June, 1895.

ing tipcat one Sunday afternoon when a voice from heaven, as searching as that which startled Paul on the road to Damascus, arrested him in his careless career. The green is probably the scene of Vanity Fair, and on it stands the curious old structure known as the Moot Hall. The whole estate was once a royal manor, and this hall the courthouse where tenants under the crown came to pay their fines.

Bunyan's Cottage, Elstow.

The upper part is now used as a chapel and schoolhouse, where services are maintained by the Bunyan Meeting of Bedford, of which Dr. Brown has been pastor for thirty-two years.

As we climbed the worn steps of the steep, narrow stairway and entered the ancient hall where Bunyan's voice had sounded two and a half centuries ago, a beautiful scene presented itself. The ladies of the parish had tastefully festooned the heavy oaken beams, bearing traces of Perpendicular carving, with delicate green vines and wild flowers and loaded tables with heaping baskets of great luscious strawberries and other food, to which we did ample justice, though it was less than three hours since breakfast. Happening to discover that it was the birthday of our genial host, three rousing cheers were given in his honor, and after the meal he held us spellbound with an inimitable address on the romance and history of the neighborhood. He related an amusing anecdote of a person who once mistook him for the author of "Pilgrim's Progress" and asked if he had written any books since that!

A visit to the parish church followed. The fine Norman arches still remain

The Moot Hall, Elstow.

of the original edifice, which is surrounded by picturesque, ivy-covered ruins of the old monastic buildings. The house of the abbey must have been new when Bunyan was a boy and altogether the most imposing he had ever beheld. He would see it

The Book of the Pilgrimage

Bunyan's Cottage at Elstow, where his Married Life began — the Garden Door.

The Pilgrims in Bedford

ELSTOW. The Village Green. — " The House Beautiful." — The Church.

The Book of the Pilgrimage

plainly as he came across the fields to church, and undoubtedly this suggested the idea of his House Beautiful, which is described in the Progress as a little apart from the wayside. As we traversed this very pathway, the June sunlight flecking the meadows wherein sheep were quietly grazing, and listened to the inspiring words of our Greatheart, we seemed to be on the Delectable Mountains and could almost see

> Over the river and in at the gate,
> Where for weary pilgrims the angels wait.

Returning to Bedford another ovation awaited us in the lecture hall of Bunyan Meeting, where a bountiful repast was served and accompanied by the usual speech-making. The massive bronze doors of this edifice are quite as beautiful as those on the Baptistery at Florence, which Michael Angelo declared worthy to be the gates of Paradise. These consist of ten panels, illustrating scenes from the Progress, and were a gift from the Duke of Bedford at a cost of over eight thousand dollars. One panel represents Slothful and his companions resting on the ground in attitudes of indescribable laziness. Here, too, we saw many interesting relics, among them Bunyan's will and an old oaken door belonging originally to the county jail in which he was imprisoned.

Rev. John Thompson.

Bedford is also famous for being the residence of the great prison philanthropist, John Howard, a statue of whom stands in one of the squares. It is a curious circumstance that of the twelve ministers who have served this church, which was founded in 1650, during the Commonwealth, seven have borne the cognomen of John. Howard's name is further immortalized by being attached to the church of which Rev. John Thompson is pastor, and the good people of this parish, not to be outdone by Dr. Brown, entertained us at afternoon tea in their pretty chapel, specially carpeted and furnished, and charmingly decorated with flowers. Between whiles some of us took a row on the "Ouse's silent tide," and others passed an hour as the guests of the two Mrs. Rose in their lovely gardens. How the English do revel in flowers, and how little the ordinary tourist knows of the beautiful home life that goes on behind the high brick walls which invariably enclose their gardens! Among our pleasantest memories are the tea drinkings and social converse within those green bowers filled with the fragrance of roses. As Dr. Brown aptly remarked: "Such visits are the best of treaties, stronger than armaments, and perpetual sureties of peace between the two great English-speaking nations." And among the cherished souvenirs which several of the party carried away from Elstow, that "quaint, quietly nestling place, with an old-world look upon it," were copies of Dr. Brown's Life of John Bunyan with the author's autograph inscribed on the fly leaf.

It was one of the days when all our hearts were touched with poetic feeling,

The Pilgrims in Bedford

but to Miss Burnham only was given the inspiration of poetic expression in this graceful farewell to him who was both Greatheart and Interpreter on this memorable occasion. With characteristic modesty the hastily scribbled verses were tucked into his hand as we separated at the railroad station, and how we gained possession of them is "another story!"

> Good-by! good-by! to pick and choose
> In courtly phrase our tongues refuse,
> The homely words of wont and use
>   Are all we try.
>
> Good-by! good-by! we may not stay:
> We touch your hand and turn away,
> But you have touched our hearts to-day.
>   Good-by! good-by!

Dr. Brown, in the course of his address in the Moot Hall, said:—

John Bunyan, who was born in 1628 and died in 1688, lived through sixty years of a memorable time in English history, and in those sixty years he wrote something like sixty books. While some bore the stamp of his genius, if there were three which stood out pre-eminently as works of genius, he should say they were the "Grace Abounding," "The Holy War," and "The Pilgrim's Progress." "Grace Abounding" is a marvelous record of religious experience, and they could hardly realize how Bunyan came to write the "Pilgrim" until they had read the other work. Dr. Duncan, of Edinburgh, used to tell his students that there were three great books of religious experience, Augustine's "Confessions," Halburton's "Memoirs," and Bunyan's "Grace Abounding," but that the tinker's book was the greatest of the three. One could not read it without feeling that it was written as with a pen of fire. It depicted the marvelous struggle of the soul through darkness up to light. The "Holy War" was a record of Christian experience of a later time, as was also "The Pilgrim's Progress." Bunyan's books went straight to the hearts of other people because they came straight from his own heart. He was his own pilgrim, and knew what it was to go through the experience which he had himself related, but if his "Pilgrim's Progress" was a dream it was a very wide-awake one. Even a man like George Jacob Holyoake said that it was a book which was homely without being vulgar, devout without being fanatical, and pointed to other worlds without ceasing to be human in this. . . . After dwelling at length upon the teachings and happy inspirations of Bunyan and his works, Dr. Brown concluded with the following lines, which appeared in *Punch* in 1874:

> To deal with the past is of small concern;
> That light for the day's life is each day's need,
> That the Tinker-Teacher has sown his seed;
> And we want *our* Bunyan to show the way
> Through the Sloughs of Despond that are round us
>   to-day;
> Our guide for straggling souls to wait
> And lift the latch of the wicket gate.
> The churches now debate and wrangle,
> Strange doubts theology entangle;
> Each sect to the other doth freedom grudge,
> Archbishop asks ruling of a judge.
> Why comes no pilgrim with eye of fire,
> To tell us where pointeth Minster spire;
> To show — though critics may sneer and scoff —
> The path to "The Land that is very far off"?
> The People are weary of vestment vanities,
> Of litigation about inanities;
> And fain would listen, O Preacher and Peer,
> To a voice like that of this Tinker-Seer,
> Who guided the Pilgrim up, beyond,
> The Valley of Death and the Slough of Despond,
> And Doubting Castle and Giant Despair,
> To those Delectable Mountains fair,
> And over the River, and in at the Gate,
> Where for weary Pilgrims the Angels wait.

The Pilgrims in London and Reigate

THE Hotel Cecil on Victoria Embankment was the caravansary at which rooms were reserved for *The Congregationalist's* party while in London, and never were plain pilgrims more sumptuously housed. The view from the balcony on the riverside at night was simply entrancing. Just across the green stretch of gardens rolled the Thames, twinkling with lights from the lazy, lumbering barges, and the fussy, flying steamers. To the right loomed up the majestic towers of Westminster and the Parliament Houses, while on the Surrey side rose the ghostly towers of Lambeth Palace. Away round the crescent to St. Paul's on the left was one unbroken sweep of bridges, moving vehicles, glimmering lanterns of all colors, and forests of shipping, making, in the weird moonlight, a scene of unparalleled beauty. The hotel was opened only last May, has more than a thousand rooms, and is superb in all its appointments. During our stay the proprietors kept the Stars and Stripes flying from the cupola. The site is historic, the original house being built by Robert Cecil, first Earl of Salisbury, Queen Elizabeth's famous secretary. From here she passed along the Strand to St. Paul's, to return thanks for the vanquishment of the Armada by her hardy sailors.

Rev. Wm. Mottram.

Sharp, indeed, was the contrast between this palatial pile and the places we visited the day after our arrival, under the guidance of Rev. Andrew Mearns, secretary of the London Congregational Union, and Rev. William Mottram, who has made a study of sites connected with Nonconformist history. The party filled two large "breaks," with four prancing horses attached to each, and attracted no small degree of attention as we drove through "this grand, imperial town," halting at places where our fathers in the faith languished in filthy prisons or gave up their lives at the stake. Two of the jails Dickens has immortalized in "David Copperfield" and "Little Dorrit." Not a vestige of one remains, and the other is now a tin-plate factory. We passed the old Tabard Inn of Chaucer's day, now a corner gin palace, and explored the gigantic modern brewery where once the bishops of Winchester had their palace. To it was attached the Clink Prison, whence the noble army of

The Pilgrims in London

martyrs went forth to the flames in Smithfield. An overwhelming sense of the preciousness of our Congregational history possessed us as we saw where Penry was hanged, when we stood within the Pilgrim Fathers' Church in Southwark, founded in martyrs' blood in 1592, and when, at the close of the day, we came to the beautiful

Memorial Hall, London.

Memorial Hall, occupying the site of Fleet Prison, in whose foul cells many Protestants and Nonconformists were confined in the days of the Tudors and Stuarts.

And what a meeting we had there! Dr. Guinness Rogers presided and alluded to the defeat in Parliament, that very day, of the Education Bill. Hugh Price

The Book of the Pilgrimage

Hughes, when speaking of it, awakened the enthusiasm of his listeners, but when he pointed to the Union Jack and the Stars and Stripes everywhere intertwined about the room and exclaimed, "That flag and that must never meet on a field of blood!" the burst of prolonged applause was thrilling in its intensity, the audience springing up and shouting with uncontrolled enthusiasm. Mr. Whittemore made the introductions in inimitable fashion, each pilgrim rising in response to his or her name. Occasional slips of the tongue, like calling for Miles Standish in place of Mr. Littlefield, his lineal descendant, caused much merriment. Ian Maclaren was expected to be present, but was detained in Wales, so sent a letter. Among the guests whose presence was felt to be a special compliment was Thomas H. Gill, author of the noble hymn, "We come unto our fathers' God." He is a man of benign learning, nearly blind, but so interested in The Pilgrimage that he allowed his weight of years to be no hindrance to being present. Fine music, an hour of social intercourse, and light refreshments constituted other features of this delightful reception.

Thomas H. Gill, Esq.

If we did less justice than usual to the delicious bread, butter, strawberries, and beverages, it was because we had just come from a tea in the chapter house of St. Paul's, as guests of the archdeacon, Dr. Sinclair, who had previously conducted us through the cathedral. He reminds one of Phillips Brooks in his tolerant spirit, as well as in his magnificent physique. This was apparent when he said to Dr. Newman Hall, as we sipped our tea in the old oak-paneled room, "If the laws and customs of our church allowed, I should be only too happy to invite my friend here to preach in St. Paul's." No other ecclesiastical building in London is so well frequented, the audiences each week day ranging from four hundred to seven hundred, and on Sunday evenings they reach five thousand. We were impressed when we attended service earlier in the afternoon with both the size and the character of the congregation, a large proportion from the humbler classes in society being present. After meeting Dr. Sinclair the secret of his influence was understood. One of the exceptional advantages which we are enjoying on this trip is the contact with leaders of thought like himself, who intersperse with their valuable talk on history or architecture a vast amount of pertinent comment on present-day problems. The outlook on the social and industrial conditions of England and America to-day, as seen from the standpoint of earnest preachers, both within and without the Establishment, is an education in itself.

Archdeacon Sinclair

At Westminster Abbey, too, storied windows, sculptured marbles, royal tombs,

The Pilgrims in London

The Cathedral Church of St. Paul, London.

The Book of the Pilgrimage

and historic monuments were interpreted to us in a fashion unknown to Baedeker by Dean Bradley, who conducted us first to the Jerusalem Chamber. As we sat in the mellow afternoon sunshine around the table where the Revision Committee met in 1870 and where the Assembly of Divines, after five and a half years, formulated their famous catechism, the long procession of sovereigns, from William the Conqueror to Victoria, who have gone out from this building to their coronation seemed to pass in review before us. We saw, in imagination, the death of Henry IV before the ancient fireplace, so dramatically portrayed by Shakespeare; and as we followed our genial and fascinating host through chapel, chapter house, and cloister of this British Walhalla, the very dead seemed to become alive through the realism of his descriptions. In the chapel of Henry VII the tombs of the two queens, Mary and Elizabeth, divided, yet side by side, taught its own impressive lesson. Although one life went out "on the black-draped scaffold," and the other "broke on old age's wheel," yet both indeed

Dean Bradley.

> Felt the thorns in the rim of the crown
> Far more than the sweep of the ermine
> Or the ease of the regal down.

Jerusalem Chamber, Westminster Abbey.

The Book of the Pilgrimage

Rev. F. B. Meyer.

Dr. Newman Hall.

Naturally our interest centered around tombs and effigies of the Tudor and Stuart sovereigns, and the dean's delightfully sympathetic allusions to Pilgrim and American history were not the least acceptable part of his informal lecture and eloquent comments.

Another enjoyable occasion was a restful afternoon tea at Christ Church, by invitation of Rev. F. B. Meyer and Dr. Newman Hall. It was a thoughtful courtesy, after a most fatiguing day, to omit speech-making and allow us the simple "fellowship of kindred minds." So we broke bread together and mingled our prayers and songs in the daintily decorated chapel where Mr. Meyer, on different days in the week, meets various groups of people, the Boys' Brigade at one time, the mothers at another, and so on through the network of activities of this flourishing church, to which, on Sunday evening, workingmen flock by the hundreds. "There is where I get my inspiration when I enter the pulpit," said the pastor, as we stood in the little entrance room, fragrant with memories of Rowland Hill. And he pointed to a photograph of Dr. A. J. Gordon on one side and to a frame on the other inclosing a leaf from the notebook of McCheyne. Between these two he would pass to his own wonderful ministry from the pulpit occupied nearly forty years by Newman Hall.

Among purely social courtesies extended to us was a garden party at The Firs, the home of Mr. and Mrs. Halley Stewart, members of Dr. Guinness Rogers' church in Clapham. By a happy coincidence the church was celebrating its two hundred and fiftieth anniversary, and we had an opportunity to meet many eminent Nonconformists. Tables with refreshments were spread under the trees on the spacious lawn, and a party of boys from the Spurgeon Orphanage furnished charming music with hand bells. Mr. Stewart is an ex-member of Parliament and holds quite progressive views on all social questions. Both he and his accomplished wife, by using their beautiful house and grounds in behalf of the sick, the poor, and unfortunate, are

Mrs. Halley Stewart

Halley Stewart, Esq.

fine exponents of the creed that wealth should be used for the blessing of others.

One of several unexpected pleasures during our stay in London was an invitation to breakfast with Lady Henry Somerset at Reigate Priory. Plans for sightseeing in the great metropolis were gladly abandoned for such a rare privilege, and an hour's railroad ride brought us to the historic spot. We were cordially welcomed by her ladyship, by our own distinguished countrywoman, Miss Willard, and her secretary, Miss Gordon, in the grand entrance hall. After being escorted by them through several rooms on the ground floor, an elegant breakfast was served in the wainscoted dining-room, which opens by French windows on to the lawn. The

The Priory, Reigate.

scheme of decoration in this room is singularly effective, the richly carved oak panels having been brought from an old monastery in Venice. Above the wainscot was a projecting shelf ornamented with jars of costly faience, once the property of Venetian monks and the repository for their drugs, the Latin names of which were curiously inwrought in the ware. The crystal chandelier depending from the ceiling was also Venetian, of exquisite coloring and marvelous delicacy. Three tables were required for our party, a large round one in the center, magnificently decorated with La France roses, and two small ones at one side.

After breakfast our gracious hostess again conducted us through the rest of the house and over the extensive grounds. Many of the trees were planted by Sir John Evelyn, the accomplished writer whose book entitled "Sylvia" was famous in its

The Book of the Pilgrimage

day. By his knowledge and enthusiasm he attracted the attention of the entire nation to the importance of planting trees. Near the house stands the chapel in which Lady Henry conducts daily service for the household. The inscription over the doorway is copied from one on the Taj Mahal and reads: "This world is a bridge, pass thee over it but build not on it. This world is one hour, give its minutes to thy prayers, for the rest is unseen." The Priory is a perfect treasure house of rare old portraits, wood carvings, tapestries, armor, statuary, plate, and all that goes with an inheritance of noble birth and great wealth. In the drawing-room is Anne Whitney's noble bust of Miss Willard.

The history of the place dates back to the days of Magna Charta, and it is believed that the prior and monks who helped the illiterate barons prepare that immortal document carried on the work in caves still to be seen near by. An ancient tithing barn, between four and five hundred years old, is preserved as an interesting relic, for here a tenth of the produce was brought by the farmers of the surrounding community to the monks as their portion. The place is also full of literary interest. Usher's famous Chronology was written at the Priory, where he died. He was afterward buried in Westminster Abbey. Not far off are the homes of George Meredith, the novelist, and Grant Allen, the brilliant essayist. Lady Henry inherits Reigate from her distinguished ancestor, Lord Somers, a marble bust of whom, in his official robes, stands at the great entrance to the House of Commons. He was the noblest and most influential patron of letters in his day.

Lady Henry Somerset.

But the place of all others which impressed us most, as Christian pilgrims, was when we stood with reverent feet beneath the tree where Lady Henry went through that wonderful subjective experience in the garden of Reigate, which changed the whole tenor of her life and placed her in the vanguard of modern reformers. Until that memorable hour beneath the elm tree in 1885, when she heard a voice distinctly say to her, "My child, act as if I were and thou shalt know I am," she had mingled freely in the fashionable and aristocratic society of London, although she herself affirms: "I have never been a worldly woman. I never saw the day that I would not gladly have left parks and palaces for fields and woods." She had been reading books more or less skeptical, and was brooding over those deep questions of life and duty which come to every thoughtful soul, when this voice of God spoke to her inmost spirit. Rising from her rustic seat, she walked to the Priory, and sitting by the window in the twilight pondered the meaning of the message. That evening she took her long neglected New Testament and read the gospel of John at a sitting. The sweet and holy revelations of that hour wrought a marked transformation in her character, and from that time onward her life has been consecrated to noble ends.

The Voice heard under the elm is still leading her up the heights of even larger

The Pilgrims in London

usefulness in connection with her latest scheme, the Industrial Farm Home in Duxhurst. An estate of one hundred and eighty acres has been secured near Reigate by the British Woman's Christian Temperance Union, where habitual women inebriates can be treated. There are little groups of cottages in six different settlements. On the theory that inebriety is a moral disease and to be treated as such, six patients are placed in each cottage under the care of an experienced nurse. This experiment in trying to check the increase of drunkenness among women is attracting much attention in England, and an effort is being made to secure an appropriation from government for the farm colony.

Still another unexpected favor was the invitation, accompanied by complimentary tickets for the best seats in the house, from Wilson Barrett, to see his remarkable play, "The Sign of the Cross." It was really a sermon on the stage, showing

Wilson Barrett, Esq.

the simple, reverent lives of the early Christians against the lurid background of Nero's court. Barrett himself personates a young Roman prefect who becomes a follower of Jesus from seeing the singular loveliness of Mercia's character. She is one of the Christian maidens imprisoned for their faith, and the part is played by Maud Jeffries with delicate reserve and deep religious feeling. The two martyrs go hand in hand to their doom, preferring

Miss Maud Jeffries.

death to a denial of their Saviour, with a sublimity of faith that is most impressive. Very sweet and tender, too, are the scenes where the Christians meet for worship in dungeons or solitary places, and the whole drama deepened our sense of what the Pilgrim Fathers must have endured in the way of persecution only a few centuries later.

On Sunday we enjoyed the novelty of hearing a sermon in the evening specially addressed to ourselves by one of London's most famous preachers, Dr. Joseph Parker, whose eloquence and originality attract immense crowds to the City Temple. In Islington, also, at the church to which the late Dr. Allon ministered, the services were arranged with special reference to our presence in the city by the present pastor, Rev. William H. Harwood. Dr. Richardson, of the party, preached in the evening for Dr. Guinness Rogers' people in Clapham, and during the afternoon several pilgrims interested in social problems visited the People's Palace and investigated the Whitechapel precincts.

Not least among the unusual courtesies extended during our stay was the

The Book of the Pilgrimage

permission, for gentlemen only, to attend sessions of the House of Commons and House of Lords secured by *The Congregationalist* through the courtesy of the Speaker of the House and Gentleman Usher of the Black Rod. It was doubtless a rare privilege for them to see the faces of party leaders whose names are as familiar as those of our own Congressmen, but the ladies bewailed the restrictions which kept them out of the Lower House. We might, it is true, have gone into the House of Lords and heard a debate on the deceased wife's sister's bill, which has come up in Parliament periodically since 1842, but we preferred a live issue! Besides, we remembered the witty saying that it is so difficult to hear in the House of Lords that members go out and buy an evening paper in order to learn what the debate is about. However, we all had a most enriching five days in London, "the buskined stage of history . . . the heart, the center of the living world."

Dr. Joseph Parker.

THE PILGRIMAGE PARTY had the pleasure of again meeting Mr. Gill, the poet mentioned in the account of the Memorial Hall meeting, at the celebration in Gainsborough. Referring to that occasion, *The Christian World* said: "An interesting figure at Gainsborough on Monday was that of the venerable hymn-writer and student, Thomas Hornblower Gill, with his snow-white hair and impressive face. Though approaching his eightieth year and apparently nearly blind, he evidently shared with keen enjoyment the spirit of the day. Two of his hymns were included in the program of the proceedings. Mr. Gill was once described by Dr. Freeman Clarke as 'a more intellectual Charles Wesley.'"

The following hymn was sung at the corner-stone ceremony at Gainsborough and also at the impressive meeting held in "The Old Meeting House," Norwich, the last night before the party left England: —

We come unto our fathers' God;
  Their Rock is our Salvation;
The Eternal Arms, their dear abode,
  We make our habitation:
We bring Thee, Lord, the praise they brought;
We seek Thee as Thy saints have sought
  In every generation.

The Fire Divine, their steps that led,
  Still goeth bright before us;
The Heavenly Shield, around them spread,
  Is still high holden o'er us:
The grace those sinners that subdued,
The strength those weaklings that renewed,
  Doth vanquish, doth restore us.

The cleaving sins that brought them low
  Are still our souls oppressing;
The tears that from their eyes did flow,
  Fall fast, our shame confessing;

As with Thee, Lord, prevailed their cry,
So our strong prayer ascends on high
  And bringeth down thy blessing.

Their joy unto their Lord we bring;
  Their song to us descendeth;
The Spirit Who in them did sing
  To us His music lendeth.
His song in them, in us, is one;
We raise it high, we send it on —
  The song that never endeth!

Ye saints to come, take up the strain,
  The same sweet theme endeavor!
Unbroken be the Golden Chain;
  Keep on the song forever!
Safe in the same dear dwelling place,
Rich with the same eternal grace,
  Bless the same boundless giver!

— *Thomas Hornblower Gill.*

Photographed by Elliott & Fry, London.

The New-World Pilgrims at The Fi
with their Hosts, Mr. and Mrs. Halley

The Pilgrims in Canterbury

SUCH an embarrassment of riches awaited us in this ancient city, seat of the metropolitan see of all England, that one's pen halts in the effort to give any adequate account of our sojourn there. Rev. W. E. Stephenson and others met us at the station and conducted us to the Congregational Church, which was packed with one of the most cordial audiences we have met anywhere. While being shown to the front seats reserved for our use, the familiar strain of "America" sounded from the organ, which is the finest in the city, with the exception of that in the cathedral. The church, founded in 1645, has a noble history. For some time it celebrated the Lord's Supper in the chapter house of the cathedral, being granted the use of the sequestrated communion plate. The members were scattered by the persecution following the famous — or infamous — Conventicle Acts, the pastor and many of his flock fleeing to Holland.

After brief religious exercises an elaborate address of welcome, beautifully engrossed, was read and then presented to Dr. Dunning. This was signed by the ministers of all the Free Churches in Canterbury, including the officers of the old Huguenot church, whose services have been held in the crypt of the cathedral for three hundred years.

"We felt we must do something," said the chairman, "to signalize the event of your visit, and decided to greet you with this address from brothers and sisters of the same belief, the same country, and the same speech." What more graceful or fitting welcome could have been offered? Rev. Morton Dexter voiced our appreciation in a brief, earnest reply, and there was opportunity, when coming out, to exchange hand-clasps with these warm-hearted friends and give individual expression to our sense of obligation for their great kindness.

Rev. W. E. Stephenson.

Next we were whisked off to St. Martin's, a quaint little edifice perched on a high hill in the suburbs, down which descended the band of Roman monks, bearing aloft the cross and chanting their Christian songs in a strange land. For here Augustine came to convert heathen England, and here Queen Bertha had a chapel fitted up for Christian worship, this being the condition of her coming to England. Her pagan husband, King Ethelred, was won to her faith and baptized in the old stone font still to be seen, so that the very stones are eloquent in history if not in sermons. Roman tiles of a dull red color are plainly discernible amid the shale and rubble, and the impression of antiquity is deepened by the old yew trees in the churchyard and the ivy-covered tower. The fascinating story of those far-off days and the subsequent history as told by the rector, Rev. L. J. White-Thomson, was a literary treat never to be forgotten. As we came away we noticed Dean Alford's grave with the touching inscription, "The inn of a traveler on his way to Jerusalem."

After a substantial luncheon at the County Hotel we wended our way to the hoary cathedral, being received first in the deanery gardens by Dean Farrar, with Mrs. Farrar and others of the household, including Dorothy, the little queen of

St. Martin's Church, Canterbury.

hearts, a winsome granddaughter of two or three summers. Would that it were possible to reproduce the scene as we grouped ourselves there in nature's court around our prince of hosts and listened to his fervent words. The keynote of his utterance was in these sentences: "Nor is my welcome to you less warm because you are Congregationalists. We differ in our views about ecclesiastical polity. We agree in our acceptance of eternal verities. That about which we differ is evanescent and, by comparison, infinitesimal; that on which we are agreed is essential and eternal."

It was like walking in a dream to follow him afterward through the gardens of the old monastery, to enter Queen Bertha's gate and traverse the very path of Chaucer's story-telling cavalcade. But when we went into the cathedral itself, a huge and complicated pile of masonry, exhaustless in its historical interest, and listened to the

The Pilgrims in Canterbury

matchless word-painting of the dean, we felt that we had reached the acme of traveling privileges. It was scarcely less a favor to have the companionship of the eminent antiquary, Canon Scott Robinson, who shared the duties of guide. Whittier's suggestive line,

> We, too, are heirs of Runnymede,

came instinctively to mind as we halted at the tomb of Stephen Langton, the great promoter of the struggle which ended in obtaining the Magna Charta.

We thought of the splendid pageants, the royal marriages, coronations, funerals, and processions of foreign kings and ambassadors which those crumbling walls had witnessed. But two spots in particular laid hold upon our imagination — the shrine of Thomas à Becket and the magnificent tomb

Dorothy at Queen Bertha's Gate.

The Deanery, Canterbury.

The Book of the Pilgrimage

The Cathedral Church, Canterbury.

The Pilgrims in Canterbury

of the Black Prince. The former, it is true, is leveled to the ground, but the pavement stained with the blood of the ambitious prelate remains, and in storied windows above may still be read the legend of miracles wrought by St. Thomas in days when king and peasant trod those aisles

The holy blissful martyr for to seeke.

The stone steps are hollowed by knees of those who knelt in penitence and prayer, or like Henry II "offered rich silks and wedges of gold" in expiation for sin. What a travesty upon the text of the archbishop's Christmas sermon, "Peace on earth, good will to men," preached only the Sunday before, was this unholy murder whose echoes are heard across seven centuries!

But the devouring hand of time has not despoiled Edward's tomb of its essential features, and we thought of that other June day, five hundred and twenty years earlier, when the greatest of the Plantagenets lay dying in the palace at Westminster and was buried in pomp in the undercroft of the church he had loved from childhood and chose for his last resting place. On the iron rod which supports the canopy are a few faded and tattered relics, the crimson velvet surcoat, the helmet, cap, and gauntlets which he wore in battle, and the red leather scabbard belonging to the sword which Cromwell is charged with having taken away. Here under the symbols of his victories lies the prince clad in complete armor, with knightly spurs at his feet, his hands clasped in prayer and on his breast the golden lilies of France mingled with the lions of England. At the base of the monument is a French inscription giving his titles in full.

Dean Farrar.

All the romantic incidents connected with his marriage to the "Fair Maid of Kent" came freshly home to us on being told that in the cathedral treasury is still preserved the original charter by which he endowed two chantries in the crypt to celebrate this episode in his eventful life. The bill legalizing the union with his beautiful widowed cousin was issued by the Pope on condition that these chantries should be founded, and in the days of Erasmus they so glittered with jewels that he cried out with wonder at the display of more than royal splendor. These vanished long ago and there is scarcely a trace of color or gilding now to be seen on the vaulted roof.

The archbishop's throne was another object which set in motion a train of historic reflections. Ninety-three primates of all England have sat in this ancient chair, but the tombs of only fifteen are to be seen in the cathedral, for since the Reformation burial has been elsewhere. Will the day ever come when the old-time custom of interring the archbishops in their own cathedral will be restored? There

The Book of the Pilgrimage

was also pointed out a low mausoleum of gray stone in which are the ashes of John Morton, the primate in whose household that handsome, manly boy, Thomas More, spent part of his youth, and in the prime of life was beheaded on Tower Hill. The head was set upon a pole on London Bridge, but a loving daughter, by bribing the executioner, secured the precious relic and had it buried in St. Dunstan's in Canterbury. Thus wherever our eyes wandered there were suggestions of strife and cruelty, of decay and death, which vaguely depress the spirit. The resplendent shrine of Becket utterly destroyed, his bones burnt and scattered to the four winds, the lights quenched in jeweled lamps, the sanctuary turned into a stable by Cromwell's rude hands, schism in the body of Christ itself — what is the lesson to be learned from events such as these? Pessimism may have its ready reply, but optimism discerns that the imperishable riches of a Christian faith still glorify every part of the huge structure, and songs of pilgrims still reverberate among the lofty pillars and arches. This was our dominant thought on passing directly from our tour of inspection to the afternoon service conducted by the dean, when we joined our English friends in singing,

> We are not divided,
> All one body we,
> One in hope and doctrine,
> One in charity.

After the service, by which we were all soothed and uplifted, some of the party were entertained at tea in the deanery, thus adding a crowning pleasure to a day of enjoyment along the highest levels. Next June the thirteen hundredth anniversary of the cathedral will be celebrated, and Dean Farrar has long been busy in making suitable preparations for the august event.

Fourteenth Century Pilgrims to Canterbury.

The Pilgrims in Boston

COLERIDGE when asked which of Shakespeare's plays was the best replied, "The one you read last." The same principle applies to the places we are visiting on this marvelous pilgrimage. Every night we exclaim, "Surely, nothing can exceed to-day's experience!" but the next morning we fare forth to new scenes equally inspiring. If our halt in a given city is for only a few hours, its hospitable citizens contrive to condense the enjoyment of days into that brief time. This was notably the case at Boston, that bustling borough on the banks of the Wash, which Baedeker styles as "perhaps chiefly interesting from its association with its famous namesake on the other side of the Atlantic." But we found it a spot of genuinely intrinsic interest, and in few places have we been more profoundly stirred by associations with our early history.

Rev. David Barnett.

Rev. W. Blackshaw.

We have now become so accustomed to distinction that it no longer takes away our breath to be met at the station by civic and ecclesiastical dignitaries and carried off in triumph to guildhalls and cathedrals. Nevertheless, "custom does not stale" nor time "wither the infinite variety" of either their welcome or our pleasure in being received. Enthusiasm, therefore, was at concert pitch when Rev. D. Barnett, Rev. W. Blackshaw, and others of the Free Churches greeted us as we stepped from the railway carriages and escorted us to the Peacock and Royal Hotel, where the mayor, the vicar, and other friends joined us at the substantial luncheon spread by mine host of this old tavern. For a wonder we had eaten only one breakfast since rising, consequently we were in prime condition to do justice to the tempting viands. The addresses which followed from Mayor Clarke, J. W. Smith, representing

The Book of the Pilgrimage

the Nonconformist churches, and the vicar, Rev J. Stephenson, were more than ordinarily cordial, and both Dr. Dunning and Hon. J. A. Lane made felicitous responses.

These agreeable functions over, the party proceeded to St. Botolph, the noblest parish church in all England, which boasts

> The loftiest tower of Britain's isle
> In valley or on steep.

It is modeled after the one which crowns Antwerp cathedral and looks forth "far over leagues of land and leagues of sea." When we reached the chancel all joined in singing the familiar hymn,

> O God, our help in ages past,

and in repeating the Lord's Prayer, led by the vicar. The focus of interest, however, was the Cotton Chapel, which has been restored by New England Bostonians in memory of John Cotton, who, when appointed vicar, was told by the Bishop of Lincoln that he was "a young man and unfit to be over such a factious people who were imbued with the Puritan spirit." How little the bishop dreamed that the youth would subsequently become famous as a Puritan of the Puritans! Mr. G. S. W. Jebb, author of a delightful history of the church, explained its chief features, and a copy of the book was presented to each of the party.

A hurried visit followed to the old Guildhall which stands in a street containing the queerest of riverside warehouses. In the ancient courtroom with its wagon roof, wainscoted walls, and list of mayors since 1545, Brewster and his companions were tried. We descended the narrow stairway down which the Pilgrims were conducted into the dark cells un-

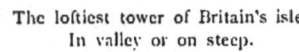
Rev. John Stephenson.

St. Botolph's Church, Boston.

The Pilgrims in Boston

derneath, where they were confined by English magistrates for attempting to leave their country after they had been harried out of it! On'y two of these gruesome chambers now remain. A mild sensation was created when our esteemed "lineal descendant," Dr. Robinson, was thrust into one of them by the military member of our party, General Wheeler, but his period of incarceration was not long. The striking contrast between the spirit of the seventeenth and the nineteenth centuries was pertinently put by one of the local papers in this wise: "Very different was the reception of the modern pilgrims compared with the experiences of their ancestors. As on that memorable day nearly three hundred years ago, they were somewhat a spectacle of wonderment to the multitude. But instead of repairing privily to a lonely place by the tidal river they were driven publicly through the streets to the leading hostelry; instead of arrest and ill treatment, they were met with nothing but kindness; instead of a prison, a banquet. In one matter the visit resembled that of old days; having once set foot in town, the visitors found it difficult to tear themselves away."

Among the ten New England Bostonians in the party were some who could lay no claim to the distinction of having ancestors who came over in the Mayflower, and such felt a pardonable pride in the consciousness that here, at least, a link was established with the Puritan past in a common name for the two cities,

> Which binds with an atoning power
> Two great and kindred lands.

Three hours was a meager amount of time to devote to such an interesting old city, but at the expiration of that time we were whirled off to Lincoln, richly laden with beautiful memories of St. Botolph's town.

The Pilgrims in Lincoln

DURING the railroad journey of a little more than an hour to Lincoln we wondered if we could possibly absorb any more enjoyment that day. But the greeting at the station by Rev. J. D. Jones, the able pastor of the Newland Church, was irresistible, and after dinner at the White Hart Hotel we all promptly appeared at the County Assembly rooms for another demonstration fully equal to anything lavished upon us elsewhere. The mayor, Councilor E. Harrison, in the full splendor of his official robes, with the mayoress, ministers of all denominations, and prominent citizens, making a total of over three hundred persons, gathered in the handsomely decorated rooms for the usual round of speechmaking, interspersed with music, refreshments, and that social intercourse which has given us such favorable opportunities for becoming better acquainted with our English cousins. A fine large engraving of the Departure of the Pilgrims was placed among the flags and flowers. The formal address of welcome, read by Rev. Z. Robinson in behalf of the Lincoln Free Church Council, was inscribed on vellum, richly bound in morocco leather, and bore the city arms with the motto,

Rev. J. D. Jones.

Floreat Lindum. This beautiful souvenir will undoubtedly be placed on exhibition in the Congregational Library at Boston. Dr. Dunning in his reply quoted most effectively a sonnet of T. B. Aldrich's, which had just appeared in the July *Century*, closing with this prophecy concerning the attitude of England and America: —

> Thy blood makes quick her pulses, and some day
> Not now, yet some day, at thy soft behest,
> She at thy side shall hold the world at bay.

Mayor of Lincoln.

The elegance of all its appointments and the high social standing of many of the guests mark this entertainment as among the finest arranged in our honor. An amusing little episode was when the mayor's chamberlain, an important functionary in a red coat with gilt buttons, who presented the guests as they entered, rapped us to order in the middle of the evening, ascended the platform and solemnly called out, "I claim your silence and attention!" We supposed this was the herald for something quite extraordinary, and were rather taken aback when he held up to view a lost fan and asked for the owner.

Sunday mercifully intervened before another week of social excitement, but two of the party, Rev. Messrs. Soule and Leete, preached in Lincoln pulpits, while Rev. L. L. Wirt was in great demand for Sunday-school addresses. As loyal Congregationalists we have made it a point — and considered it a privilege — to attend Nonconformist churches in the morning. In the afternoon we have generally worshiped in the cathedrals. This happened to be Coronation Sunday, and the anthem appropriate to the day was a notable feature of the evening service. As a few of us lingered to enjoy the magnificent organ music at the close, there transpired another of those pleasant surprises which have marked this trip from the outset. The sub-dean, Dr. Clements, who had previously sent us his card with the offer of any courtesy in his power, came forward and hospitably urged our going to the deanery close by to see the commanding view from the hill, on which portions of an old Roman wall are still in a good state of preservation. He then took us into the house, and again we had a glimpse of a lovely English home, with its indescribable air of repose and cultivation. Our host manifested especial pride in calling attention to the old gallery staircase running around three sides of the entrance hall, also to the carved bookcase in the library which

Congregational Church, Lincoln.

he had had made to order when a student at Oriel College, Oxford. As we entered the drawing-room an elderly lady of sweet and gracious mien advanced from a recessed window, the very place, she told us, where Bishop Paley was accustomed to sit when writing his "Evidences of Christianity." A pleasure analogous to this was a visit Monday morning to Monks' Manor, the elegant home of Joseph Ruston, D.L., a former M.P., who has a superb private art gallery, rich in paintings of the Rossetti school, which was freely opened for our inspection.

The Monday morning service at the cathedral included a most intelligent rendering of Mendelssohn's "If with all your hearts," by tenor solo and chorus, which was greatly enjoyed by the pilgrims, on account of whose presence the anthem had been

The Book of the Pilgrimage

The Cathedral Church, Lincoln.

The Pilgrims in Lincoln

selected. After the service we examined in detail the unsurpassed beauties of the majestic edifice under the scholarly guidance of the sub-dean, who mentioned the fact, as particularly interesting to Puritans, that Cromwell's soldiers did not show their accustomed zeal in disfiguring the minster at Lincoln. This was explained on the ground of having a mayor in the height of the vandalism of those times who, though a Puritan himself, did not justify such outrageous manifestations of religious fervor.

Among the points of special interest were the tombs of St. Hugh, the industrious pioneer of early English architecture, and of Remigius, the first bishop of Lincoln, who in 1075 began "a strong and fair church" which was "both pleasant to God's servants and, as the time required, invincible to his enemies." The angel choir which Freeman cal's "one of the loveliest of human works," the chapter house of surpassing beauty, the monument of Queen Eleanor, lately restored by Mr. Ruston, and the fine old thirteenth century glass windows were other attractive features fluently described by the sub-dean.

Not the least valued experience of the morning was the hour spent in the library with the cathedral librarian, Rev. A. Maddison. An original copy of Magna Charta was a document of absorbing interest, recalling

Sub-Dean Clements.

> With what an awful grace those barons stood
> In presence of the king at Runnymede,

on that eventful June day six centuries agone, and wrested from his reluctant hand that great charter of human rights. The meaning of history presses upon us more and more as we pursue our pilgrim way and we find ourselves echoing the lamented laureate's lines : —

> Yet I doubt not thro' the ages one increasing purpose runs,
> And the thoughts of men are widened with the process of the suns.

The Pilgrims in Pilgrim Land

HOWEVER much we have felt the preciousness of our Congregational faith in other places, perhaps the most abiding impression of its value came to us the day when we drove from Lincoln to Gainsborough. It was a glorious morning, the horses were in fine fettle and our route lay through a region replete in Nonconformist history. When we reached Gringley-on-the-hill a bevy of children waving a small American flag saluted us by the wayside. From this eminence the little town of Epworth, the cradle of Methodism, is plainly visible, and the entire landscape, with its wealth of green hedgerows, waving fields of grain brilliant with poppies, noble trees and winding streams, was spread before us in a panorama of loveliness.

With reverent feet we wended our way first to the old manor house in Scrooby, where Brewster was born. It is indeed one of the ironies of history, as Dr. John Brown points out, that the house where the archbishops of York had found a home for centuries, where Wolsey had lodged and from which Bishop Bonner had dated his letters, became for the Separatist church the house of God and the gate of

The Approach to Scrooby.

heaven. These great houses, surrounded by a moat, must have been very stately and beautiful in their palmy days. Probably nothing finer existed in the way of domestic architecture, but scarcely a vestige of their former grandeur now remains. It was difficult to imagine Elizabeth and other sovereigns halting here on their royal progress up to Scotland, or the great Wolsey spending weeks in retirement beneath

The Pilgrims in Pilgrim Land

The Manor House, Scrooby.

its roof. But little cared we just then for the doings of kings and cardinals. The one grand figure which loomed up from the past was the elder of Plymouth Colony, whose memory we shall revere anew after standing on ground hallowed by his feet and within the humble parish church in which he was baptized. The baptismal font has been removed to the New England Church in Chicago, but the carved oak which formed the Brewsters' family pew and other objects of interest are still to be seen.

They must have been people of good social standing, for William Brewster, as

A Scrooby Inn.

well as his father and grandfather, filled the office of postmaster in the old manor house, a position of no small honor in those times. Until the reign of Henry VIII there was no regular system of posts in England, and for long after that the only four that were established were for the exclusive use of the sovereigns.

Halting at Bawtry for a second breakfast, we pushed on next to Austerfield, the birthplace of William Bradford, and again the past wove its magic spell about us. Impressive, indeed, was the quaint little church with its old Norman font, used for a time as a pig trough, but reclaimed from such base uses not long ago by the parish vicar. The restorations now in progress will rescue the fine Norman arches from the modern wall built into them on one side of the church, and when the work is completed this ancient house of worship at Austerfield will be one of the interesting relics of the Norman period.

The Bradfords, too, must have been well-to-do, for they belonged to that sturdy yeoman class which, in Elizabeth's reign, stood next to the gentry, and the future governor of Plymouth Colony was reared in a house which possessed a library of English and Latin books; no insignificant sign of prosperity when books were rare and costly. One of the objects of peculiar interest which occupied our attention was the old register in the church which records his baptism on March 19, 1589.

But the culminating point of all our journeying seemed to have been reached when we descended into the cellar of the humble Bradford cottage where, doubtless, the early Pilgrims convened to worship, as did the Christians of the first century in the Catacombs. We can imagine with what heavy hearts plans may have been laid here for leaving the mother country. Fifteen of us, perhaps, crowded into the little cell-like inclosure, and we felt the presence of saints from the Celestial City as we sang,

O God of Bethel, by whose hand
 Thy people still are fed,
Who through this weary pilgrimage
 Hast all our fathers led,

and the tender, fervent prayer of Dr. Richardson

The Church at Scrooby.

The Pilgrims in Pilgrim Land

The Market Cross, Bawtry.

The Book of the Pilgrimage

The Church in Austerfield.

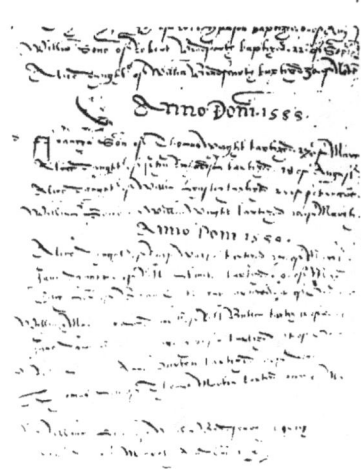

Record of Bradford's Baptism.

brought us still closer to the heart of the Eternal.

A graceful feature of the drive that day was when we were arrested at a pretty cottage by the wayside, not with hostile intent, but to present each pilgrim with a basket filled with fresh roses and strawberries, and a bunch of forget-me-nots daintily laid on top. We were indebted to Mrs. G. S. Lister, of Finningley Park, for this graceful courtesy. Her thoughtful bounty provided the flowers and fruit which she sent thus to intercept us on our pilgrimage. How beautifully symbolic was the offering of all that has been done for us in

This land of such dear souls, this dear, dear land,
Dear for her reputation through the world!

The flowers faded with the day, but the deed will be forever enshrined within our grateful hearts.

The Pilgrims in Pilgrim Land

Austerfield.

Bradford Cottage Austerfield.

The Book of the Pilgrimage

The Old Hall, Gainsborough.

Luncheon in the Old Hall, Gainsborough.

The Pilgrims in Pilgrim Land

These rich experiences of the morning formed a fitting prelude to the grand occasion in the afternoon at Gainsborough. This is an attractive old English town, the scene of "The Mill on the Floss," St. Oggs, along whose banks Tom and Maggie "wandered with a sense of travel," being none other than the Trent The town was gaily decorated, and the British and American flags were everywhere displayed. The presence of many distinguished English guests, as well as Ambassador Bayard, drew a throng of people from the neighboring towns, and it was an imposing scene when the Urban District Council, on a raised platform in front of the Town Hall welcomed the ambassador. The square was packed solidly full, the windows of surrounding shops were filled with eager faces, and shouts rent the air at the conclusion of the address and responses.

J. F. Bayard

We then adjourned for luncheon to the Old Hall, one of the most picturesque structures of its kind that we have seen in all England. For several centuries it was the residence of the lords of the manor, and there is reason to believe that the church to which John Robinson ministered held services there. It is certain that Wesley preached in the banqueting hall, but the house ceased to be used as a dwelling about one hundred and fifty years ago. Within fifty years it has been restored by the present owner, Sir Hickman Bacon, who claims descent from the great Francis, and through whose hospitality we were permitted the rare privilege of feasting beneath its ancient roof. Oriental hangings adorned the walls, and over the windows were curious armorial devices. Alderman Joseph Thompson, of Manchester, presided at the luncheon and proposed the first toast to the Queen. All rose and sang a verse of the national hymn, and in rising we heard murmurs from several loyal subjects of "The Queen, the Queen! God bless her, God bless her!" Earl Brownlow, in proposing the toast for the President of the United States, alluded felicitously to the historic event which had occasioned this international gathering, and spoke of his personal association with James Russell Lowell, when he was ambassador at the Court of St. James. He also quoted this apt after-dinner utterance made by Mr. Lowell when the American Rifle Team competed at Wimbledon : " If ever

The Book of the Pilgrimage

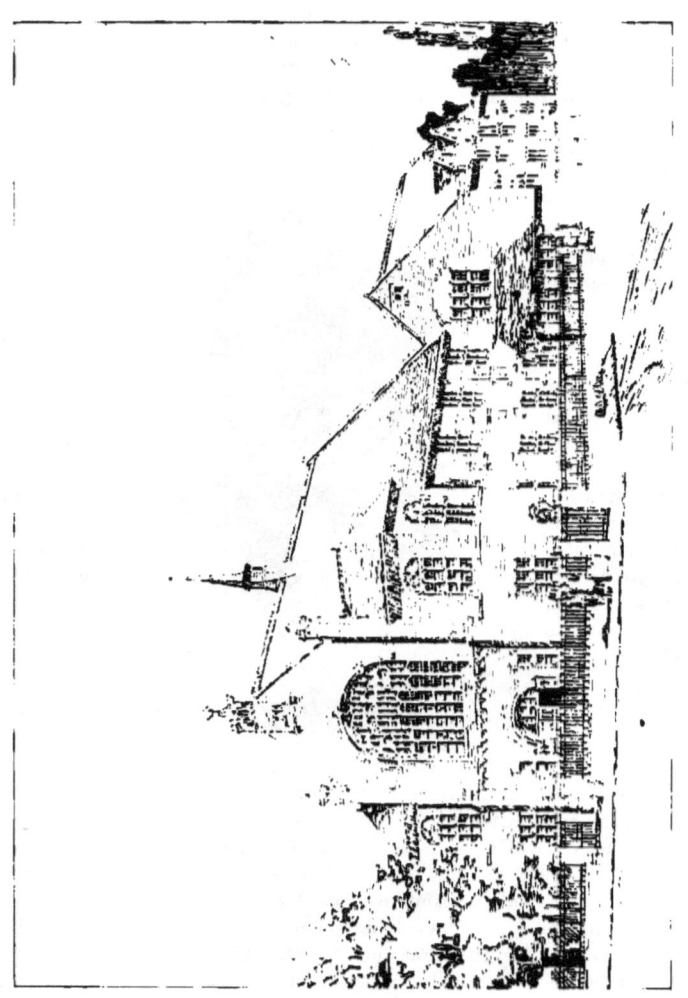

John Robinson Memorial Church, Gainsborough.

The Pilgrims in Pilgrim Land

the riflemen of both nations should be fated to meet in battle, may God grant that the rifles of both nations may be turned in the same direction." The sentiment was enthusiastically applauded, thus giving fresh evidences of the strong anti-war feeling that has found expression on so many occasions since our arrival at Plymouth. Another outburst of cheering reverberated along the oak gables of the Old Hall when Ambassador Bayard, in his reply, said with much fervor: "It means a great deal when we from both sides of the Atlantic meet together, and with all sincerity of feeling drink to the health and long life of the rulers of each of our countries. May the time never come when the health of the ruler of Great Britain and the health of the chief magistrate of the United States may not be drunk with the same good feeling that we each and all of us do to-day."

Rev. H. S. Griffiths.

The next objective point was the site of the new John Robinson Memorial Church, whither we marched in a body, accompanied by civic authorities in official robes, denominational leaders in academic cap and gown, Sunday-school children with banners, and the Britannia band. The crowd had augmented, if possible, and a passage for us was kept clear, not by armed sentinels, but by little girls holding a rope of ribbon. Rev. H. S. Griffiths, the pastor, who has worked heroically to secure the building now to be erected, had general charge of the services. Platforms were erected for the speakers and members of the Sunday-school, and Rev. J. Morlais Jones, chairman of the Congregational Union of England and Wales, presided. A feature of the devotional services was the singing of this hymn, written for the occasion by Rev. W. T. Matson, of Portsmouth: —

Father, to thee this fare we raise,
  In memory of a sainted soul;
  His mind was free, his heart was whole,
    Be thine the praise!
His witness to the truth and right
  Abides, a quenchless day-beam shed
  Upon us, from the fountain-head
    Of heaven's own light!

No menaces of hostile power
  Availed with him, to hold back aught
  The Word disclosed, or bind his thought
    Enchained an hour.
And for his latest testament,
  He bade us keep an open mind,
  Assured the wealth Thy Word enshrined
    Might ne'er be spent.

For him, and all who like him priest,
  Before us, toward the mark, be told
  Our God's high praises, while we hold
    Their memories blest!
Oh, may their mantle on us fall!
  And may thy grace our souls endue,
  That we may live our lives as true,
    And free from thrall!

And from this house we build for God,
  Long may the glory of the Lord
  Shine out, and his victorious Word
    Sound forth abroad;
Battling with error, vice, and sin,
  Casting down every evil thing
  Abhorred of God, till Christ shall bring
    His kingdom in!

The Book of the Pilgrimage

The distinguished writer of religious verse, Marianne Farningham, who is rarely seen in public, occupied a seat on the platform, and her strong, sensitive face, framed in a wealth of gray hair, evinced a keen enjoyment of the exercises. These lines from one of her poems were not inappropriate to this gathering: —

> To-day the Lord's disciples serve in throngs,
> And they exult because of long-past night;
> They sing triumphantly their victor songs,
> And push their way along new paths of light.

Rev. Hugh Griffiths presented Mr. Bayard with a silver trowel, a gift from the Gainsborough church, ornamented with a design of the Mayflower, also a scene representing Robinson kneeling on the beach in prayer with his fellow pilgrims before leaving Delfshaven. With this beautiful implement he performed the ceremony of laying the corner stone. The difficulty of hearing in the open air detracted from the enjoyment of the ambassador's admirable speech, but fortunately it was printed in full in all the local papers. The dedicatory prayer — a remarkable and impressive utterance — was offered by Rev. W. J. Woods, after which Dr. Mackennal delivered a short address, and Rev. Morton Dexter spoke a few words as representative of the National Council of the American Congregational Churches. An enthusiastic mass meeting at Wesley Church in the evening, at which Albert Spicer, M.P., presided, and Dr. Guinness Rogers, Rev. C. A. Berry, Dr. Cyrus Richardson, and others spoke, closed the exercises of this phenomenal day.

A town which carries the trace of its long growth and history like a millennial tree, and has sprung up and developed in the same spot between the river and the low hill from the time when the Roman legions turned their backs on it from the camp on the hillside, and the long-haired sea kings came up the river and looked with fierce, eager eyes at the fatness of the land. In these words George Eliot described Gainsborough, the town of "The Mill on the Floss," to which she gave the name of St. Oggs, making reference also to that bit of its history which interests us most to-day, of the time when honest citizens lost all their possessions for conscience' sake, and went forth beggared from their native town. Here are houses standing now on which they turned their backs in sorrow, quaint gabled houses looking on the river, jammed between newer warehouses, and penetrated by surprising passages, which turn at sharp angles till they lead you out on a muddy strand, overflowed continually by the rushing tide! It was to this town that "New-World Pilgrims to Old-World Shrines" came on Monday, drawn thither by the fascination of a name, that of the man who, though he did not himself sail away to America in the Mayflower, was the teacher and inspirer of those who did. — *Marianne Farningham, in The Christian World.*

The Pilgrims in Pilgrim Land

THE FULL TEXT of the address delivered by Hon. T. F. Bayard, the American ambassador to the Court of St. James, in connection with laying the foundation stone of the John Robinson Memorial Church at Gainsborough, June 29, is given below:—

We have gathered here — many of us from lands far distant and beyond the great seas, and many more from English homes closer to the scene — to lay the corner stone of a memorial church, which is intended to be a monument dedicated to the glory and worship of Almighty God and the loving memory of his faithful servant, John Robinson, of Gainsborough-upon-Trent, in northwestern Lincolnshire, who, not far from the spot where we stand, was born 320 years ago, and whose body was returned to dust at Leyden, in the Netherlands, in the year of our Lord, 1625 — as is there recorded upon the mortuary tablet in the Church of St. Peter and St. Paul in that city. Nothing, as it seems to me, could be less worthy and more unfit than to make this an occasion for the vainglory of rhetoric, and by interposing the commonplaces of oratory and verbal decoration to deprive the noble simplicity of the life and character of John Robinson of its own native force and impressiveness. If we can only realize or imagine how the man himself would have felt if living here to-day among us, we will be in a frame of mind which will better enable us to comprehend him and the lesson of his life, and appreciate the fruits of his works, which "do follow him." In such a spirit and with such intent I shall endeavor to say the few words which I have been asked to say by reverend ministers of the Congregational order in my own country — a request seconded by the reverend ministers who represent the union of Congregational churches in Great Britain.

THE PURITAN REVIVAL.

The "emancipation of England from Norman domination" I believe to be a just and true title and description of the spiritual movement of which, on the threshold of the seventeenth century, the scanty handful of simple agriculturists at the neighboring "townlet" of Scrooby, on the River Idle, near its junction with the Trent, was the nucleus, of which John Robinson became the pastor, and whose place of worship was the hall of the manor house of William Brewster, who was born at Scrooby — the only member of wealth in the congregation and a graduate of the University of Cambridge. Of the birth and parentage of John Robinson, whose exile began when he was thirty-one years old and was lifelong, there remains but vague history; for, owing to his enforced separation from this country, and the prelatical persecutions that at that time desolated the homes and families of all independent religious dissidents, but little has survived of documentary proof of the local and personal history of the period, so that I have not been enabled to discover even the names or residences of his progenitors, or trace collateral relationships. Of his own career in England, as afterwards in Holland, happily there is no room for doubt; and his own hand has left the written record of his thoughts and labors in the cause of "soul liberty" and emancipation, which have borne such fruits in both hemispheres of the globe. That he himself styled Lincolnshire "his county," and thence proceeded, at the call of conscience, after he had withdrawn from his ministry in the national church at Norwich, may be held to fix that county as his place of birth. At the age of seventeen his name is found enrolled in the University of Cambridge, and on the register of Emmanuel College is entered as a sizar, March 2, 1592; took his degree M.A. in 1600, and B.D. 1607. I am aware that the register of Corpus Christi College also contains the entry of his name — John Robinson, E. Lincolnshire, admitted 1592, and Fellow 1593 — and perhaps the date of his degree of B.D. in 1607 in the register of Emmanuel may leave an open question as to this last entry.

THE CHARACTER OF ROBINSON.

But he completed his terms at Cambridge, where his scholarship gained for him a fellowship and the highest honors that university could bestow; and he truly was, in the words of a contemporary, "learned, polished, modest, and not easily to be paralleled." We find that his four years of ministry at Norwich were filled with unrest and mental disquietude, and that in 1604 he withdrew to Lincolnshire, and there united himself with a congregation at Scrooby who had constituted themselves into a church by a solemn covenant with God and with each other—"to walk in his ways made known, or to be made known, unto them according to their best endeavors, *whatever it should cost them*." From Ashton's Memoir of John Robinson, and annotations, I here transcribe:—

"Scrooby must henceforth be regarded as the cradle of Massachusetts. Here the choice and noble spirits, at the head of whom were Brewster and Bradford, first learned the lessons of truth and freedom. Here, under the faithful ministration of the pastors, they were nourished and strengthened to that vigorous and manly fortitude which braved all dangers; and here, too, they acquired that moral and spiritual courage which enabled them to sacrifice their homes, property, and friends and

The Book of the Pilgrimage

expatriate themselves to distant lands rather than abandon their principles and yield to the attempted usurpation in the liberty of their consciences."

And let us not, I pray you, allow our sense of sympathy for such men to degenerate to the lower level of mere pity; for indeed they had that within them which placed them in life, as it does their memories to-day, quite above and beyond the need of such an emotion. John Robinson and his co-religionists trod the winepress of affliction, but they trod it with a lofty spirit, with the moral dignity of sublimated intent. They were filled with that joy which is born of a cherished conviction in its hour of oppression, and which seems for its perfection to need the sharp frosts of adversity, such as approaching winter brings to the American forest, giving tints of an autumnal beauty more exquisite than the luxuriance a summer sun can ever bestow. Such men never crept, but ever marched through life— "*Anthropoi*"—with heaven-erected faces, and heard ever singing in their hearts the clear, uplifting voice of judicial conscience, like a trumpet call to the clear spirits, for they felt themselves soldiers in the cause of truth and heard her accents in every vicissitude. My dear countryman, James Russell Lowell, in a preface to a Life of Izaak Walton—a contemporary (although a little younger) of John Robinson—describes as the "sixth beatitude" that "the pure in heart shall see God, not only in some future and far-off scene, *but wherever they turn their eyes.*" And by this we may be able to comprehend what it was upon which the minds and hearts of these pilgrims and their pastor were fed, and upon what they turned their eyes and found cause for hope and cheerful courage in the dark hours of their persecution, adversity, and affliction. The religion of assent has its equal counterpart in the religion of dissent—the obligation to do those things that we ought to do and the equal obligation to leave undone those things we ought not to do.

OUR DEBT TO BYGONE GENERATIONS.

Is it not well to pause now and then on our journey and consider the indubitable progress of civilization, the actual moral outgrowth of the principles of Christianity and the consequent advance the world has made under it, and how to-day we accept and enjoy, as a matter of course, the blessings and advantages of civil and religious liberty, giving but little thought to the generations who in bygone years toiled and suffered to secure them for us? How small the measure of our gratitude and infrequent our recognition of those who

Beyond their dark age led the van of thought!

On such a scene, and on such an occasion as this, well may the words of Whittier be repeated:—

> . . . We lightly hold
> A right which brave men died to gain;
> The stake, the cord,
> The axe, the sword,
> Grim nurses at its birth of pain.

Consider the absolute and unquestioned religious liberty of the times in which we live and in those countries governed by the English-speaking races. And then go back three hundred years and endeavor to realize here in England the condition of John Robinson and his little flock of co-religionists at Scrooby, asking only to be allowed to worship God and lift their hearts to him in such words and forms of supplication for his guidance and mercy as their needs of conscience and the instinctive hunger of the heart instructed them to pray for.

INDIVIDUAL FREEDOM THE ROOT OF SOCIAL AND RELIGIOUS PROGRESS.

Conscience and reason were the underlying moral forces, then as now, at work, and from them was slowly evolving all social and political progress, at the root of which lay the recognition of individual freedom and "the equal right of every man to be unhindered by men in the fulfillment of his duty to God." Yet in those days, under the reign of James I,—a pedantic bigot, well styled "a captain of arts and a doctor of arms,"—it was forbidden so to pray in England, and equally restrained were they from going out of England to pray in foreign lands. It was sought to enforce the royal claim to settle the world's theology by the will of a monarch, to make the religion of the magistrate the religion of the people; and all individual freedom of conscience and mind was to be despotically coerced into unintelligent or hypocritical submission. The Christian religion was not based upon worldly power or property in any of its forms, but upon freedom of conscience, and the kingdom of God had been divinely declared to be within each human heart. The principles of such a system, of necessity and logically, brought into active exercise those qualities of mind and moral nature which were thus developed naturally and instinctively—the muscles of the mind which, like the muscles of the body, are educated into strength, and both obey the same inherent natural law of growth by use; and thus it is plainly seen how liberty leads to strength and the health of the body politic. But the terrible and momentous issue was raised whether liberty of conscience was to be allowed, or were men to be forced into atheism or become utterly irreligious, or compelled to a sacrilegious reception of the sacrament

— no true conversion, but the deadly sin of hypocrisy and the desecration of what is holiest.

A TRIBUTE TO THE DUTCH PEOPLE.

When such an issue was framed the morality of John Robinson and his associates, founded on religious principles, could not hesitate. And, as William Bradford has recorded, "being thus molested, and with no hope of their continuance there, by a joynte consent they resolved to goe into ye low Countries, where they heard was freedom for religion for all men." This was in 1607, and I will not recite the sad and well-known history of the arbitrary and cruel measures that were resorted to to prevent the departure of the congregation, and how finally, in broken detachments, distressed, despoiled, imperiled, by land and by sea, they came, after great hardships, together in Amsterdam, and in the course of another year were transferred to Leiden. And is not a tribute due here and now of gratitude and honor to the country which, in their hour of sore need, gave them welcome, protection, and generous toleration in an age of intolerance? The Netherlands was but a little patch of earth rescued from the sea, warred over by man and the elements, without natural advantages other than those arising from contact with the sea, which was ever threatening to engulf them, yet in the seventeenth century this war-worn, weather-beaten strip had become the commercial center of Europe, an asylum for the victims of religious persecution, and is one of the phenomena of history. A military eye would have sought in vain for strong natural positions; no ranges of hills, no salient features for the combinations of resistance and the delivery of assault; the breastworks of Holland consisted only in the stout hearts of her people, sustained by conscientious conviction, animated by hope and calm reliance on that Power with whom the wisdom of this world is but foolishness. In a fearful struggle, lasting forty years, it had gained its own liberties against desperate odds, with an unflinching and pertinacious courage never paralleled in the annals of history; had made its soil the grave of 300,000 invading Spanish soldiers, and compelled an expenditure by Spain of more than 200,000,000 of ducats in the futile effort to subjugate it — the vain attempt to prescribe, as Motley says, "what was to be done in this world and believed in the next." Taine says that in 1609 the Dutch Republic was two centuries ahead of the rest of Europe. Their idea was the organization of society for the public good, and this made them the instructors and civilizers of the modern world and caused their country to become a haven of safety for the victims of persecutions for opinions' sake in France and in England. More books were printed in Holland in the seventeenth century than in all the other countries of Europe put together.

THE PILGRIMS IN LEIDEN.

Unquestionably the commercial freedom, the liberality of trade in the Dutch Republic induced many Englishmen to transfer their energies and fortunes to that country; for all the branches of liberty spring from the same stock and gather strength from the same ideas. Commerce has ever been the great civilizer of mankind, for it not only teaches honesty, without which commercial dealings are impossible, but it makes intelligence essential. In Leiden the congregation remained eleven years, John Robinson having been admitted in 1615 as a member of the Leiden University, pursuing diligently his studies in theology. It is noticeable that the same tolerant and generous welcome was extended to the Huguenot refugees, who equally found asylum in Holland; and a declaration recorded by Robinson contains the interesting historical fact: "Touching the ecclesiastical ministry — namely, of pastors for teaching, elders for ruling, and seasons for distributing the church contributions; as also for the two sacraments, baptism and the Lord's Supper — *we agree in all things with the French reformed churches.*" But despite the liberty of conscience afforded by Holland, the English pilgrims were restless until they should again live under English laws, and that their children should retain the language and name of Englishmen. Their lives, too, were full of toil, and not of a kind to which they had been accustomed, for at home "they had only been used to a plain country life and the innocent trade of husbandry."

THE VOYAGE OF THE MAYFLOWER.

They felt themselves "constrained to live by leave in a foreign land, exiled from home and country, spoiled of goods, destitute of friends, few in number and mean in condition." They were undoubtedly in danger of becoming absorbed in the community around them, of losing their distinctive church organization, their national identity, their language and its traditions. And believing this, John Robinson favored the settlement, and promoted the plan for their removal to the new colony beyond the Atlantic, and measures were taken to carry it out. He made it a condition precedent of the removal from Holland to Virginia that they should not be disturbed or injured in their new homes on account of their peculiar religious practices and opinions. Not without many delays and serious difficulties was the expedition fitted out; but finally, in August, 1620, the embarkation of the congregation took place, at Delft Haven, in the Speedwell, which was to meet her con-

The Book of the Pilgrimage

sort, the Mayflower, at Plymouth, from which port, and on September 6, 1620, the two little vessels set sail. I need not recite to you how they were compelled to return to port, because the Speedwell was thought to be unseaworthy, and the Mayflower proceeded alone, bound for the Hudson River, but by stress of weather was forced northward, and with her one hundred and one passengers, men, women, and children, in stormy weather made her landing on Cape Cod on November 9. It was the intention of John Robinson to have followed, but circumstances prevented, and his death occurred a few years after; but in 1629 his sons, John and Isaac, with the remainder of the Scrooby congregation, joined in the settlement in America in which his heart was so enlisted, but which he was destined never to see.

THE OUTCOME OF THE EMIGRATION.

It is clear and plain to us now that the departure from England of this small body of humble men was a great step in the march of Christian civilization; it contained the seed of Christian liberty, freedom of inquiry, freedom of instruction, freedom of man's conscience. " Like unto a grain of mustard seed, which a man took and sowed in his field, which is indeed the least of all seeds, but when it is grown, it is the greatest among herbs, and becometh a tree so that the birds of the air come and lodge in the branches thereof." Little regard had John Robinson for worldly fortune, fame, or what goes by the general name of success. He deduced his duty from the profound principles disclosed to his personal conscience, enlightened by religion and founded on the moral order revealed to the world by the teachings and example of the Saviour Christ. His simple, unselfish, courageous life is illuminated by the principles of his divine Master, and therefore he still lives; and this is the origin of the edifice whose corner stone we lay to-day. In his Memorials of Canterbury, Dean Stanley — a kindred spirit to John Robinson — asks: —

"Had the great Stephen Langton, the cardinal archbishop, been asked which was most likely to endure, the Magna Charta which he won from John or the shrine which five years afterwards he consecrated in the presence of Henry III, he would, beyond all question, have said the shrine of St. Thomas. But we see what he could not see; we see that the charter has lasted, because it was founded on the eternal laws of truth, of justice and freedom; the shrine has vanished away, because it was founded on the passing opinion of the day, because it rested in ignorance, which was gradually dissolving, because it was entangled in exaggerated superstitions which were condemned by the wise and good, even in those very times."

And the works, the name, the fame of this simple pastor of a human flock will endure, and generations yet unborn shall seek in this church a touch of his vanished hand, a scent of his fragrant memory, redolent as it is with the sweet odor of unselfish devotion to the service of God and loving-kindness to his fellow-creatures.

JOHN ROBINSON'S NAME AND CHARACTER A TIE BETWEEN ENGLAND AND AMERICA.

He had lived not quite fifty years when he was called back to God, and on March 1, 1625, he heard "the one clear call," and, as was then written of him, "if either prayers, tears, or means would have saved his life he would not have gone hence." John Robinson, a minister of Christ, died in exile and in poverty, and to-day two great nations are represented here in paying honor and respect to his memory and moral worth. His name and character create a tie between those who feel the kindred, not merely of a common language, — the mother tongue of both peoples, — but of the thoughts and feelings of which language is merely the clothing and the symbol; and out of these thoughts have grown convictions of mutual duty, from which we cannot detach ourselves if we would — and, as I sincerely believe, would not if we could. The wide ocean he never crossed, and which lies between his grave and the colony he planted on the other side, has become a bridge, and no longer is a barrier, but serves to bring together the people of the two countries who share in love and sympathy in his life and work. His memory is a tie of kindred — a recognition of the common trust committed to both nations to sustain the principles of civil and religious liberty, of which he was a fearless champion and under which has been so marvelously fulfilled the prophecy, "A little one shall become a thousand, and a small one a great nation."

The Pilgrims in Ely

ELY, the little town in the fen lands of East Anglia, the scene of Kingsley's "Hereward," where, for a single night, the pilgrims laid aside their "staff and sandal shoon," will ever abide in their memories as a veritable Chamber of Peace. Whether or not our gracious host, Dean Stubbs, surmised that we had reached that point in our journeyings where we needed "time to repair our nature with comforting repose," his plans for our entertainment conduced wonderfully to that end. The very invitation to a "tea in the cloister garth" had a soothing sound and refreshed our jaded spirits like a rest in music.

We arrived late in the afternoon, and lowering skies and a chilly atmosphere soon drove us from the garth into the deanery drawing-room. What a lovely, reposeful, homelike interior it was, with its recessed windows, its wealth of choice pictures, its atmosphere of antiquity, and, above all, the cordial hospitality of members of the household! And what converse we had in the low-ceiled, wainscoted rooms as we lingered "over the teacups," listening chiefly to the dean as he told us a little of his theories of life, especially as related to the working classes, for whom he manifests a deep and practical interest. We had read something of the way in which, when vicar at Granborough, he divided his glebe into acre lots for the benefit of the villagers, and of the night school in his laundry for two winters in another parish, but this personal interview gave us a new conception of his work. Over his study fireplace are carved in oak these words from Goethe: *Gedenke zu leben* (Think of living). This sentence and another from the same book, "Earnestness alone makes life eternity," have served as his watchwords for many a year. In his forthcoming book, "A Creed for Christian Socialists," may be found the essence of the dean's ideas on socialism, which is that Christ should be

Dean Stubbs

dominant in all realms of living, in politics and industry no less than in theology and ethics. He believes in a spiritual unity, but not outward conformity between different branches of the Christian church, and rejoices in the opening of English universities to Nonconformists, because this common educational bond must ultimately prove a strong unifying influence. It was a rare privilege to hear themes of such import discussed by one who has been styled "the broad-minded, scholarly, terribly earnest, yet blithe and happy dean of Ely."

The Book of the Pilgrimage

The Cathedral Church, Ely.

The Pilgrims in Ely

At length, as sunset shadows appeared on the green, velvety close, we followed him into the noble minster, through the splendid Galilee porch, down the long Norman nave, pausing beneath the great octagonal lantern, through whose traceried windows prismatic colors were now shimmering, and came finally into that wonderful lady chapel with its inconceivably delicate carvings of fruit and flowers. This was one of the places, however, where we had no disposition to boast of our Puritan ancestry as we saw how their ruthless hands had shattered peerless statues and made havoc of unparalleled specimens of mediæval and classic art. All these points of architectural and historic interest were explained by the dean in his own inimitable fashion, but he had reserved for the evening the most unique feature of our entertainment in the shape of a "moonlight" organ recital in the cathedral.

At nine o'clock we groped our way to seats in the western end of the nave, the huge pillars looming up like giants on either side and the only light coming from the distant south transept. This dim illumination was ingeniously arranged to have the effect of moonbeams, softly stealing in at the clearstory windows, touching here and there with a mystical light the pillars and arches of the beautiful octagon, making of this incomparable architectural feature, which is the glory of Ely, a vision out of the darkness — a dream, beautiful enough to be dissipated by the first awakening to everyday realities, yet indeed a dream in stone, and its impression upon the entranced beholders as enduring as the stone itself. A fugitive beam of light caught now and then the hand or the violin bow of the player as he stood upon the choir steps, and we could well imagine one of Fra Angelico's playing angels with his golden nimbus just behind the screen of darkness.

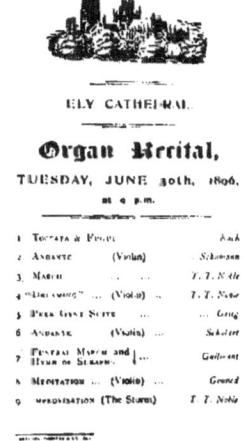

ELY CATHEDRAL.

Organ Recital,

TUESDAY, JUNE 30th, 1896,
at 4 p.m.

1	Toccata & Fugue	Bach
2	Andante (Violin)	Schumann
3	March	T. T. Noble
4	"Liebeswerb" ... (Violin)	T. T. Noble
5	Peer Gynt Suite ...	... Grieg
6	Andante (Violin) ...	Schubert
7	Festal March and Hymn of Seraphs	Guilmant
8	Meditation ... (Violin) ...	Gounod
9	Improvisation (The Storm)	T. T. Noble

Presently from out of the stillness came a message from the old master, Bach, first in soft, mellow waves of sound, creeping along the groined arches, and ending in a thunderous fugue with all the organ's power. The lofty strains died away, to be succeeded by one of Schumann's melodies on the violin, played with a power and pathos that no words can describe. Oh, the haunting sweetness of that music as it swept along the vaulted roof till it seemed as if it were caught up and echoed back by a choir of angels. One selection followed another till an hour had passed away. Then, in exalted mood, we retraced our steps, past the door where the dean stood in the shadows to receive our subdued but grateful farewells, out through the deanery gate, back to the quiet, well-kept Lamb Hotel, to lie down and dream of celestial harmonies in the temple not made with hands.

The Book of the Pilgrimage

The Cathedral Church, Norwich.

The Pilgrims in Norwich

RICH as our experiences had been heretofore, the transcendent privilege of the trip was still awaiting us at Norwich, for here was focused in a single day several of those distinctive features which had characterized the preceding weeks. The greeting from our Nonconformist brethren, full of inspiration and touching our hearts with memories of the heroism of the past and the spiritual sympathies of the present, together with all that is impressive in the architecture and pageantry of the Established Church, its clergy acting as our hosts at a grand social function, and a delightful garden party conspired to make this occasion typical of the English pilgrimage.

The ancient cathedral was celebrating its 800th anniversary, and a more imposing ceremony probably none of our party will ever see again. We were overwhelmed to find that some of the choicest seats in the building, in the organ gallery and in the choir, had been reserved for us. We supposed that our good friend Dr. G. S. Barrett, who was indefatigable in his kind services, both before and during our stay, had secured for us this exceptional privilege, but he assured us that Dean Lefroy himself had extended the courtesy. This is the more remarkable when it is remembered that we as Nonconformists represented a faith which, to a certain extent, repudiates the forms venerated by the Church of England. We had scarcely taken our seats when from the far distance came the sound of male voices, accompanied by trumpet and cornet, singing the triumphant hymn:—

Dean Lefroy.

Dr. G. S. Barrett.

Lift the strain of high thanksgiving!
Tread with songs the hallowed way!
Praise our fathers' God for mercies
New to us their sons to-day;

Here they built for him a dwelling,
Served him here in ages past,
Fixed in it their sure possession,
Holy ground, while time shall last.

The Book of the Pilgrimage

This was a token that the procession had started from the cloisters, and as the stately body moved with slow and measured steps down the nave the congregation caught up the strain and the magnificent volume of praise did not cease till the last ecclesiastic, His Grace the Lord Archbishop of Armagh, Primate of all Ireland, who preached the sermon, was seated within the altar rails. A more dignified and impressive scene can hardly be imagined. First came the civic functionaries led by the Norwich Corporation in their splendid regalia, and preceded by an official bearing the mace, glittering with beautiful rock crystals, a gift from Queen Elizabeth. Next came other mayors in the diocese in official robes and chains, members of Parliament and of the Grand Lodge of Masons, barristers in powdered wigs, officers of the Princess Royal's Dragoon Guards, and, most imposing of all, the clergy and cathedral body, wearing cassock, surplice, stole, hood of their degree, and college cap. The choir boys were in blue and white; the doctors of divinity were easily distinguished by their scarlet gowns, and the bishops by their immense lawn sleeves.

The Choir, Norwich Cathedral.

Last of all came the Lord Bishop of Norwich, before whom was borne his silver crosier, escorting the Archbishop of Armagh, the entire procession numbering nearly 400. A deeply interesting thanksgiving service followed, in which it was noticeable that a prayer for the President of the United States was included in the general collect, then a sermon showing how cathedrals may truly minister to one's spiritual life, and

The Pilgrims in Norwich

at its close a marvelous rendering of Stainer's sevenfold Amen by the choir. As the waves of almost divine harmony swept over the bowed heads of the great congregation new depths of reverence were opened in our hearts, and to worship before the Almighty seemed the very transport of human joy. During the recessional hymn the same body of ecclesiastics and other dignitaries slowly marched out of the cathedral, and the return, from our advantageous point of view, gave a fine opportunity to study their faces.

Archbishop of Armagh.

About a hundred of the more eminent guests, including nine bishops and many of the nobility, had been invited by Dean Lefroy to luncheon in a spacious marquee on the deanery grounds, and to this number he added the entire American party. This distinguishing act of hospitality, on an occasion when he might have ignored our presence in the city without the least discourtesy, shows the catholic spirit of the man. Nor was our invitation an afterthought, for among the toasts on the daintily printed *menu* cards was one to "Our Kinsmen Beyond the Sea." This was proposed by the guest of honor, the Archbishop of Armagh, Dr. Alexander, whose wife wrote

There is a green hill far away,

and other beautiful hymns, and Dr. Dunning responded in a manner that made us nowise ashamed of our leader. His Grace said he believed that the American visitors would carry back with them a message of honest, downright love from one people to another, so as to make the notion of a war between England and America utterly inconceivable. The sentiment evoked enthusiastic applause, nor was it the only expression of a similar kind during the feast. The Bishop of Norwich, speaking of the passion for freedom which had brought forth such glorious fruit in England, making it the happiest and freest country in the world, added, "Of course, I include our Anglo-Saxon kinsmen across the Atlantic." Canon Jessopp, too, eminent as an antiquarian, who has written some fascinating stories of old abbeys and friars, and is an authority on folklore, paid a fervent tribute to the founders of America, characterizing the Pilgrims as "apostles of freedom — men before their age." What a reversal of opinion since the day when some of them were "clapt up in prison and others had their

Bishop Sheepshanks.

houses beset and watched night and day" because they taught "strange and dangerous doctrine"!

    Careless seems the great Avenger . . . but behind the dim unknown
    Standeth God within the shadow, keeping watch above his own.

The Book of the Pilgrimage

The afternoon began to wane when we realized that we must surrender these social delights for a scene quite different in character but most elegant in all its appointments. Mr. J. J. Colman, the millionaire manufacturer, and the Misses Colman had arranged for a garden party in our honor to which about five hundred guests were invited. After a cordial reception by our host and his charming daughters we strolled about the gardens, which cover over a dozen acres and occupy the site of an old Benedictine priory. Parts of the original edifice are still preserved and have been transformed into a unique sort of lodge, full of art treasures and objects of historic interest.

J. J. Colman, Esq.

The fireplace in the library bears the escutcheon of Isabel Wygan, who was prioress in 1514. A few years ago the shaft of a Norman column was accidentally discovered in the gardens, and now, by the help of an expert antiquarian, the outline of the whole group of early buildings, including the church, is plainly defined.

Greenhouses filled with rare exotics, a wealth of native flowers, shady groves, winding avenues of noble trees and velvety lawns, lured us to prolong our rambles over this beautiful estate, which stands on a height commanding a superb view of the surrounding country.

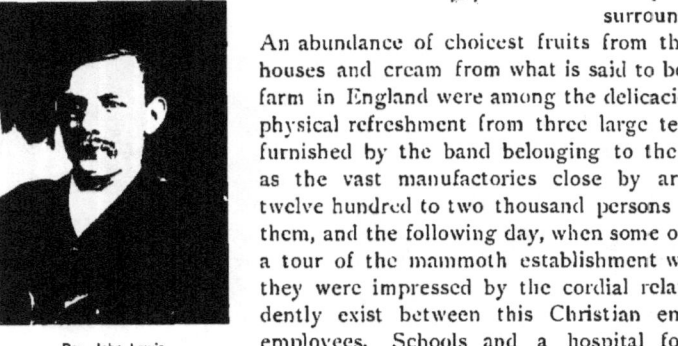

Rev. John Lewis.

An abundance of choicest fruits from the adjoining hothouses and cream from what is said to be the finest dairy farm in England were among the delicacies served for our physical refreshment from three large tents. Music was furnished by the band belonging to the Carrow Works, as the vast manufactories close by are called. From twelve hundred to two thousand persons are employed in them, and the following day, when some of our party made a tour of the mammoth establishment with Mr. Colman, they were impressed by the cordial relations which evidently exist between this Christian employer and his employees. Schools and a hospital for their use are

The Pilgrims in Norwich

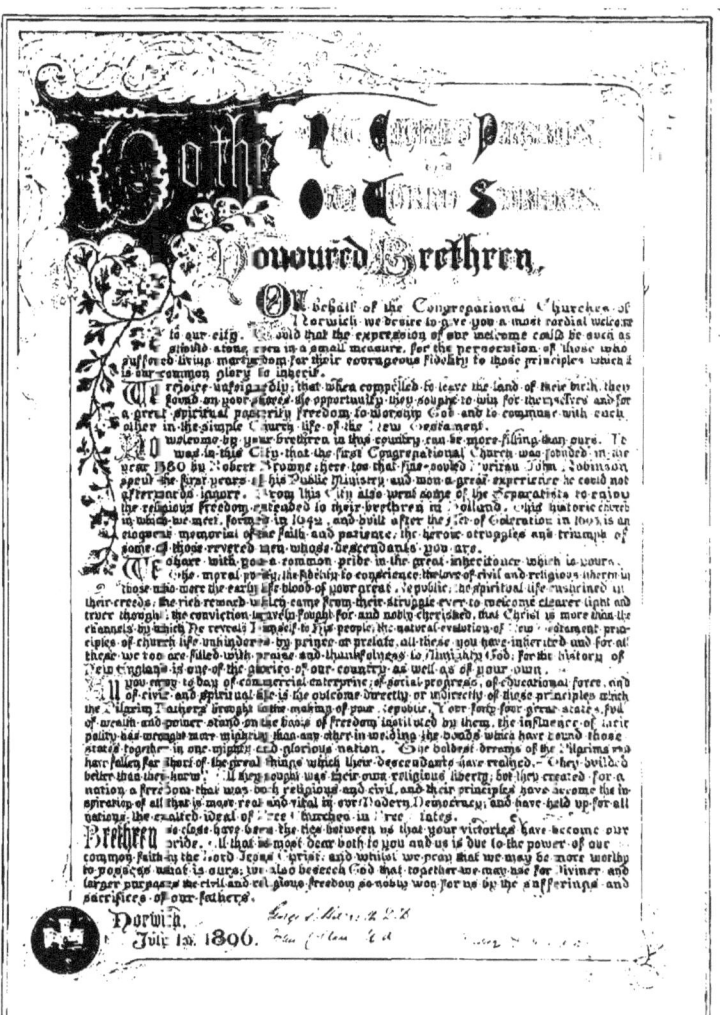

AN ADDRESS OF WELCOME.
Presented to The Congregationalist's Pilgrims in the Old Meeting House at Norwich, England.

The Book of the Pilgrimage

external signs of his devotion to their welfare, and Dr. Barrett's church, where he worships, is another object of his generous beneficence.

Full as the day had been, it detracted nothing from our keen appreciation of the evening reception in the Old Meeting House, given by our own brethren in the faith, the mayor himself presiding. The plainness of both edifice and assembly offered a sharp contrast to the splendid spectacle in the cathedral a few hours before, and thereby accentuated to our thought the cost of our religious liberty. Here was a city in which the first Congregational church was founded by Robert Browne in 1580; here John Robinson spent the first years of his public ministry, and four of the early pastors of this very church suffered bitter persecution, having been ejected from the Establishment by the famous Act of Uniformity. These and other thrilling facts were eloquently presented by Rev. J. Lewis, the present pastor, in his address of welcome, which was beautifully engrossed on vellum. Several speeches from both Englishmen and Americans followed, and we heartily indorsed the words of Dr. Barrett when he said: "This little pilgrim band will leave England with full hearts and tender memories. They will never forget the kindness and welcome extended to them on all hands; they will never forget English hearts and English homes." The next morning both he and the mayor devoted themselves to showing us points of interest about the city. We were glad to enter Dr. Barrett's own church, with its spacious Sunday-school rooms, accommodating nearly a thousand pupils, and to examine at the Guildhall the rare old silver pieces used at the corporation banquets. There were massive tankards and sauce boats, salt cellars and loving cups of quaintest designs, a rose-water bowl of delicate *repoussé* gold, all historically interesting as well as intrinsically beautiful. The Elizabethan mace already mentioned, and used only on state occasions, and the mayor's rich regalia were also seen.

Another element of pleasure during our stay in Norwich was to be entertained at the Maid's Head Hotel, which had an existence twenty years before the discovery of America by Columbus. While modern conveniences have been added, enough of antiquity remains in the shape of latticed windows, wide fire-

The Maid's Head, Norwich.

places, and old carved furniture to fascinate the visitor for hours together. The writer was fortunate in being assigned to the identical apartment occupied by Elizabeth during her visit in 1578, and one could almost believe that the old-fashioned canopied bed and the queer little ewer and pitcher were a part of the furnishings then. In the assembly room, where famous men in wigs and ruffles and noted beauties in wondrous headdresses and costumes once made a brilliant show beneath the blaze of wax candles, the diminutive gallery for the fiddlers is still preserved.

Something of the sadness — though for a far different reason — which filled the hearts of the early Pilgrims as they bade farewell to old England gave a tinge of melancholy to our departure that afternoon. The land that Shakespeare calls "this precious stone set in the silver sea" is endeared to us by a thousand new ties,

> For there runs
> The same blood in our veins as in your sons;
> The same deep-seated love of liberty
> Beats in our hearts. We speak the same good tongue,
> Familiar with all songs your bards have sung.

And sweeter and stronger than all other links in this chain of international fellowship are our common love and service for the same divine Master.

A consciousness that the time had come for the beginning of separations from each other added to our feelings of tender regret upon leaving old England. Two of our number, Messrs. Dexter and Whittemore, were to accompany us no farther, and as we brake bread together for the last time in the quaint banqueting room of the Maid's Head, at Norwich, an unwonted quiet fell upon our spirits. Dr. Richardson, General Wheeler, and others, in behalf of the party, thanked these two gentlemen for their efficient services, and each in reply adverted to the singular unity and good fellowship which had marked the trip from the outset. It is doubtful if an equal number of persons, most of whom were almost or quite strangers to each other when they embarked, ever traveled together more harmoniously. The speakers also took occasion to express the unanimous sentiment of appreciation felt by the party to *The Congregationalist's* management, both for the first conception of the pilgrimage idea and for the manner in which the elaborate plans had been successfully worked out.

Devout recognition was made of the still more remarkable circumstance that not a single plan had miscarried, from illness or any other cause, and that each individual whose name appeared on the original membership list, printed a week before leaving America, was enabled to place his or her autograph on the register of the Old Meeting House in Norwich on this last day. Mr. Whittemore, in a deeply reverent and rarely graceful speech, disclaimed the idea of any real breaking up of a party having a purpose like ours, for the sacred shrines we had visited together were a token of the eternal bond existing between Christian believers. Verily there

> Are things with which we never part;
> From clime to clime, o'er land and seas,
> We bear them with us in our heart

The Book of the Pilgrimage

Delfshaven, Holland

The Pilgrims in Holland

THE exceptionally smooth passage across the North Sea brought us, on the morning of July 3, to the mouth of the Maas, and as we sailed up the river all the picturesque features of the Dutch landscape were clearly outlined in the bright sunlight. What a fascinating picture it is, especially when seen for the first time! But if one expects to find the country precisely as it has been painted by artists, or described with so much charm by Thackeray, he will suffer a degree of disappointment. The general outlines, of course, are the same, but the trail of the tourist is over much of the land and has effaced certain features that now exist only in books or on the canvas of painters. The eternal flatness and greenness are indeed unaltered, the black Holstein cattle still graze in the fertile lowlands, shining canals fringed with tall reeds intersect the rich meadows as of yore, windmills which have flapped their unwieldy arms for three centuries continue to

In Delfshaven.

The Book of the Pilgrimage

loom up against the horizon, all life moves leisurely, and the hands on the dial of time seem to have been set back hundreds of years.

But along the towpath, where walks a man in a blue blouse and wearing a wooden yoke to which is attached the rope that draws the lumbering barges, it is not uncommon to see a bicycle spinning past. Occasionally, too, one notices a whizzing steam engine cheek by jowl with the ancient, clumsy windmill, and the conjunction seems like an impertinence. Another odd sight is a modern bonnet perched on top of the queer Dutch caps, with their spiral gold pins standing out like horns on each side of the head just below the eyebrows. The old headgear, made

In Delfshaven.

of embroidered muslin and stiffly starched, with a cape coming well down on the shoulders, is most becoming to the wholesome, dumpling-faced farmer's wife as she stands in the doorway of her green little cottage, but the modern combination is simply grotesque. In order, therefore, to satisfy one's imagination it is desirable when traveling through Holland to get beyond the urban centers into the real country where life is still primitive and where the storks, solemnly nursing one leg, have not been driven away by railways and steam trams.

Our party was reënforced at Harwich by several English friends, among them Dr. Mackennal and his daughter, of Bowdon, Rev. E. J. Dukes, of Bridgewater, and

The Pilgrims in Holland

Mr. George Hardy, of London. Dr. Mackennal, as chairman of the English coöperating committee, was largely influential in making our reception in England such a success. Mindful that our chief aim was to retrace the footsteps of our exiled fathers, we first took a carriage drive around the city, thence to Delfshaven, and saw in imagination that memorable farewell so pathetically described by Bradford. He says: "Truly doleful was the sight of that sad and mournful parting; to see what sighs and sobs and prayers did sound amongst them, what tears did gush from every eye and pithy speeches pierced each heart; that sundry of the Dutch strangers that stood on the quay as spectators could not refrain from tears."

Fourth of July was spent at The Hague, where Li Hung Chang and his suite happened to arrive at the same time, and for their accommodation we had to yield

Buying Milk.

the quarters engaged for us at the Hotel des Indes and were transferred to the Paulez. However, we had a fine opportunity to see the Celestial group and solaced ourselves with a few patriotic after-dinner speeches, "making a great deal of noise," as Dr. Park wittily remarked, "in the land of William the Silent."

In the afternoon we went to Scheveningen, an expensive watering place three miles from the city. It differs outwardly from an American seaside resort in the number of bath chairs — hundreds of them — scattered along the beach. They are of wickerwork, and in shape not unlike a magnified old-fashioned sunbonnet. In them people sit and read or doze by the hour, agreeably protected from the sun and wind. Many are decorated outside with advertisements of cocoa in huge black letters. In former years this was a good place to see the distinctive costumes of the

The Book of the Pilgrimage

City Gate, Leiden.

fisher-folk, who, alas! are fast adopting conventional garments. Thus do civilization and the influence of cosmopolitan ideas tone down much of the old picturesqueness here as in other parts of Europe.

On the Lord's Day we tarried in Leiden, where the exiles found an asylum for eleven years. The significance of Puritan history again took on a new meaning as we worshiped in the great church of St. Peter, close by the house bearing a tablet with the inscription : "On this spot lived, taught, and died John Robinson." Dr. Brown calls attention to the fact that young Rembrandt was living with his father in Leiden at this time, and there is nothing improbable in the thought that Robinson in his walks may have seen the bright-faced lad at his games, and in later years passed him as a student on the University stairs. A hospital now occupies the site, and in the afternoon we held an impressive service in a bare little room in the lodge, climbing up the frightfully steep stairs which are a common feature in Dutch architecture. The place was hot and crowded to excess, so that we stood in a double row around the walls, there being no seats. But we came to worship and to thank God for his wonderful mercy, and the thought of all present naturally reverted to the time when Robinson here preached to his devoted followers. They must have looked upon the same huge church which towered over us, and we could easily imagine what sad forebodings filled their minds, for the loftiest faith never dreamed of the glorious development awaiting their cause. Dr. Mackennal made a thoughtful, earnest address, Dr. Robinson, the worthy descendant of his pious ancestor, led us in prayer, and the exercises closed by singing,

My country, 't is of thee.

St. Pancras, Leiden.

The old university, which Niebuhr calls "the most memorable room of Europe in the history of learning," was another interesting shrine that claimed our attention, and it was pleasant to find one of our own countrywomen, Miss Putnam, of New York, a student there. She is a daughter of the well-known publisher, and enjoys the distinction of being the first American woman to be matriculated at a Dutch university. While our guest at luncheon the next

The Pilgrims in Holland

day she entertained us with a vivacious account of her life among this conservative, sturdy, and intelligent people. While here some of the party drove to Katwyk, six miles distant, where immense sand dunes pleasantly relieve the monotonous level of

Leiden — The Townhouse seen from the Burg.

the country, and where clumsy, square-prowed Dutch boats are drawn up on the beach. Beneath the shadow of their gayly painted hulls, and all along the shore, one may see wonderfully interesting types of life in costumes that for antiquity and picturesqueness far exceed those at Scheveningen. We halted for a few hours at

The Book of the Pilgrimage

Haarlem, for the purpose of enjoying a musical feast in a recital on the famous organ in the old Groote Kerk, and to visit the ancient town hall. We also loitered about the market place where an amazing lot of old rubbish was exposed for sale, together with articles of real utility and value.

In Amsterdam we were quartered at The Victoria, a fine hotel near the station and within easy walking distance of the Dam, that great central thoroughfare whence radiate streets in every direction like the lines of a spider's web. Here one finds no lack of objects to divert and amuse. Rows of high-gabled houses, some tipped at angles that give the appearance of toppling over into the canal; the somber royal palace, kept up at large expense, although the young Queen

St. Peter's Church, Leiden.

The John Robinson House, Leiden.

Wilhelmina spends only six days in the year there; the swinging drawbridges; the motley crowd showing many Jewish faces; the network of trams with windows shut air-tight even in midsummer; the bevy of old salts with pipes in their mouths sunning themselves on the steps of the Zeemanshoop (seamen's hope); the dignified Exchange, where the bloated bondholders of the city congregate at noontime, — all this and much more make a moving panorama of singular fascination. Both here and at The Hague several hours were devoted to the superb art galleries with their incomparable portraits by Rembrandt; tiny interiors, perfect in every detail, by Gerard Dou; rollicking street scenes by Jan Steen, and inimitable faces by Frans Hals, of whom some one has said, "He could paint a laugh, a

The Pilgrims in Holland

The Ferry, Amsterdam.

great boisterous, ringing, roystering laugh, as no painter has given before or since."

In Amsterdam traces of the Separatist church are well-nigh obliterated, as its members abode there less than a twelvemonth. But through Dr. Brown's fascinating book, "Pilgrim Fathers of New England," we were enabled to form a mental picture of Francis Johnson, the first pastor, "a single young man and very studious," who once "lived on ninepence a week and subsisted on boiled roots." Associated with him as teacher was Henry Ainsworth, of whom Bradford said there is "not his better for the Hebrew tongue in the university, nor scarce in Europe." We also

In Amsterdam.

recalled a characteristic incident in the life of the late Dr. Dexter during his last visit to that city. Confident that in the old Stadhuis he could find the missing record of Governor Bradford's marriage, he interviewed the custodian, who politely informed him that Professor de Hoop Scheffer and other eminent antiquarians had made exhaustive search for the names of English exiles with only indifferent success. Moreover, with a shrug of the shoulders, the official averred that such searches were "very dusty and disagreeable"! But a ten-shilling piece modified his views on that point and the precious record was found, also the only known signature of Ainsworth. The custodian was amazed and exclaimed, "How is it that you come hither 3,000 miles and in five minutes discover what our local students have all along searched for in vain?" Professor Scheffer was among the first to express appreciation of the find, and subsequently sent Dr. Dexter 118 of these valuable marriage records between the dates of 1598 and 1617.

Amsterdam— The Little Street of the Brownists.

Two delightful excursions, by means of a specially chartered steamer, were made to the Isle of Marken in the Zuyder Zee and to Alkmaar, the celebrated cheese market, which on Friday presents a scene unparalleled elsewhere in Europe. This method of travel through the canal is far and away more delightful than by rail and gives one a most satisfactory idea of the unique landscape of the Netherlands. At Marken both men and women wear bloomers of coarse woolen cloth, and the women have one or more ringlets stringing down each side of the face from beneath a close-fitting white cap. They, as well as the little girls, wear a sort of quilted, gayly decorated corset outside their cotton blouses. Heavy wool stockings and wooden "klompen" (Dutch for sabots) complete the outfit, which looks hot and uncomfortable in summer. But one is a bit disappointed with Marken, on account of the evident spirit of greed that pervades the island, and a suspicion that these costumes and manners are retained chiefly for the revenue they bring in attracting tourists. Even the youngest children have learned one English word, money, and they follow visitors from point to point,

The Pilgrims in Holland

clattering along in their klompen and holding out brown, chubby hands for coins. One expects beggars in Italy and Egypt, but not in industrious, self-respecting Holland.

At Broek, also, though for a different reason, the traveler experiences something of a shock. This is the far-famed "cleanest town in Europe," where a model dairy farm, with about fifty cows, is kept on exhibition "every day for 25 cents," as the proprietor's card reads. It is too obviously a show place to fit one's ideas of rural simplicity. People and cattle dwell together under one roof, and the stranger is expected to be properly amazed at seeing cow-stall windows draped with tiny lace curtains, and strips of carpeting laid the length of the cheese room, which is not separated, even by a partition, from the spick and span quarters of the cattle. At milking time the cows' tails are fastened out of the way to a hook in the ceiling. But these forms of cleanliness seem obtrusive and artificial.

On the Dike.

No disillusions await one, however, at Alkmaar. In the great open market place are pyramids of shining red and yellow cheeses which are counted, weighed, and then conveyed on stretchers by two men, one at each end, to barges in the canal, whence they are sent all over Europe. The men are arrayed in spotless white duck trousers and blouses, and in this case cleanliness seems normal and necessary. Each

The Book of the Pilgrimage

group of men is distinguished by a different color of ribbon on the hatband. The ancient Weigh-House is a quaint, heavily rafted structure, fitted up with scales that have done duty for more than two centuries. The whole busy scene is intensely interesting. The men step about with an alert, proud air, giving an impression of that thrift and honesty which are distinguishing features of the Dutch.

One comes away from Holland with a genuine admiration for the land and the people. Who that has seen it can ever forget the soft harmony in natural graduated grays in the landscape beloved by Dutch painters? And who can be indifferent to the pluck which has wrested their little kingdom from their natural enemy, the sea, or wrenched it from that fiercer foe, the Spaniards? Its glorious history appeals to Americans, especially to those whose ancestors found an asylum from persecution in their sea-girt land.

From this point onward our paths radiate all over Europe to Germany, Italy, France, Austria, Norway, and Sweden, and only twelve of the original pilgrims will return together to the New World.

Looking Backward

ONE day towards the last of our journeying together it was suggested that each pilgrim should mention two events or experiences which, in the retrospect, stood forth as having afforded peculiar pleasure. Naturally a large majority singled out some such exceptional privilege as being entertained at Farnham Castle by Bishop and Mrs. Davidson, or participating in the splendid celebration at Norwich. But in nearly all the testimonies it was noticeable that the chief element of joy lay in the fellowship with English people rather than in the beauties of nature or the glories of art, thus verifying what Lowell once said: "Books are good dry forage, but, after all, men are the only fresh pasture." As an illustration of some of the impressions received through this medium, witness the verdict of a Connecticut pastor:—

An evening in the study of Dr. Forsyth, pastor of one of the Congregational churches in Cambridge, and the personality of the "Congregational bishop" of Wells are noted because of a peculiar charm which belongs to a trip abroad. A century of America could not furnish two such evenings of Europe. Both men are the product of the characteristic civilization of England, yet are totally different as representing the contrasting results of differing types of conformity to the same environment. Two of the editorial staff of *The Congregationalist* furnished the open sesame to poor mortal me to the delightful suburban home of Dr. Forsyth. Mr. Dale, illustrious son of an illustrious father, completed the company. To describe what was said and done and thought is impossible. Dr. Forsyth is a Christian Chesterfield with a keenness of intellect that is perfectly delicious.

In the old, sleepy, ecclesiastical city of Wells we found dear Dr. Kightley, whose appearance is as fascinating as the cathedral, and he looks nearly as old. His very make-up of body and mind is ecclesiastical. Overshadowed in the place of worship by the great cathedral, and overshadowed in position by deans and canons, yet this true bishop of the church feeds his flock and I doubt not rules his house. To him the visit of the pilgrims was an epoch, and from his joy he seemed to say, Simeon-like, Now let thy servant depart in peace, for mine eyes have beheld the glory of Congregationalism. Bishop Ken's hymnology will hereafter have a charm before unknown, and the Doxology will have a larger, fuller, broader, and deeper meaning, due to the earnest interpretation and unique personality of this venerable servant of God.

Of our intercourse at Wells with Bishop Kennion and the simple, spontaneous service in his palace another pilgrim said:—

One deep impression was the vitality of spiritual life really uniting Established Churchman and stanchest Dissenter, emphasizing Paul's statement concerning many members, yet one body,

The Book of the Pilgrimage

and making sure the fulfillment of the day when without uniformity there shall yet be unity in the church.

In a similar vein some one else spoke of the entertainment of a part of our company in the beautiful home of Dean Farrar in Canterbury : —

After the impression of the magnificent cathedral, with the glimpse at its history and associations given by the dean, to be welcomed with sweet English courtesy to a typical English home and enjoy moments of delightful fellowship in which the oneness of those loyal to the same Master remands to fit remoteness minor differences of forms and hereditary associations, made up an hour of golden opportunity and satisfaction.

Of this same day at Canterbury and of the personality of the dean still another remarked : —

It was to me the most impressive and delightful of the whole pilgrimage because, first, the old St. Martin's Church, together with the magnificent cathedral, brought us into direct touch with early Christian history, linking the religious efforts of the present with the distant past. At no other point did ancient deeds move me as they did here. Secondly, because the bearing as well as the words of Dean Farrar charmed me. He seemed in reality the wonderful man I had thought him to be. Before I left home I had anticipated the day here as the climax of the pilgrimage and the privilege it would afford of seeing and talking with a man whose written words have greatly moulded my thought.

The object of our pilgrimage and the extraordinary welcome accorded us on account of it were repeatedly emphasized in this retrospective analysis. The formal addresses of welcome were sometimes beautifully engrossed on vellum or parchment. Some idea of them may be formed from the accompanying illustration, a reproduction about one quarter size of the one presented at Norwich, but the embellishments in gold and the tasteful coloring of the initial letters are necessarily lost in the reproduction. The mild sensation which our coming sometimes produced is reflected in a humorous little episode told by one of the ladies. She begins, however, by saying : —

I saw nothing anywhere more affecting and impressive than this universal welcome from Mr. Maxwell, the first to board the Columbia from the tender at Plymouth, to the Mayor of Norwich, who bade us good-by outside the castle gates. We could never forget that we were not common sight-seers. Our purpose to honor those who suffered for our sakes was an open sesame to doors and hearts at every step along the way. It is in that character that sweet and gracious courtesies were extended to us, who else, many of us, must have been totally unrecognized. Even the poor folk paid unconscious tribute to the motive which actuated our visit. Streaming down Pin Lane in Old Plymouth little children peeped at us with wondering finger in the mouth. At last, in a quaint old doorway, a decrepit grandam spoke the thought we afterward heard expressed in so many varying tones of kindness : " Eh, child, look well on 'em. They 're dear folk, Lord bless 'em ! They 're the American Congregationalists ! "

> Avenge, O Lord, thy slaughtered saints !

cried Milton in his immortal sonnet. Was not this a most sweet avenging?

Looking Backward

The warmth of greetings at the other extreme of the social scale is well typified in our reception by the master of Trinity College, Cambridge, which a lay member of the party thus describes: —

This visit to the master's lodge was one of the pleasantest, because, first, it was so unusual a favor, granted seldom to Englishmen, still less to the average tourist. But the greatest charm was that Dr. Butler received us with such hearty, unaffected cordiality that we forgot we were strangers and pilgrims, and had for an hour or two the sensation of feeling ourselves distinguished guests. Along with his entertaining and instructive explanation of portraits and historical souvenirs, he made such frank and affectionate allusions to his own home life and friends that we felt we had received a double honor in being let into the heart of both the lodge and its master.

This serene and loving atmosphere, which is characteristic of English home life, and of which we had many inspiring glimpses during the summer, is one of the most charming pictures that many of us will have to hang on memory's wall. Speaking of the afternoon at Bemerton, a New England lady said: —

To pass from that tender service in George Herbert's church into the quiet rectory, a nest of contentment, then through the drawing-room windows to the lovely garden with its outlook on trees, river, lawn, and fields, was the blissful hour of my pilgrimage.

Two others particularly enjoyed the Sunday afternoon which a few of us spent with Mr. Henry Tolson and his wife on their fine estate, Park House, in the suburbs of Exeter.

Shall I ever forget, asked one, the picture of sweet domesticity which was unfolded to our view as we drove through the gates and saw that family group on the lawn? Our gracious host and hostess met us, not afar off, but on the very doorstep, and took us at once into the household circle gathered on that stretch of velvety greensward. A high wall, over which a wealth of roses clambered, screened them from the street, and in this bower of beauty and fragrance we sat and talked on themes suited to the day, while the children amused themselves quietly about us. There were nine of them, all under fourteen. What pretty names they had, and with what childish grace they told them to the American strangers! We wrote them down in memory's book — Ruth, Margery, Phillis, Jack, "Sunny," otherwise Joseph, Roger, Barbara, Ronald, and Hugh. A well-worn copy of Waugh's Sunday Afternoon Readings for Children, with which the mother had been entertaining the older children, lay upon the table. Tea with clotted cream, from vessels of rare old silver and china, was served out of doors, together with thin slices of buttered bread, buns, and simple cakes, which the children passed around with the help of only one maid, for in this Christian home as little service as possible is required of the servants on the Lord's Day. The afternoon sunlight flickered through the trees and lay in golden beams athwart the meadow stretching beyond the gardens. It was all so quiet and peaceful, so sincere and unpretentious, that I could not repress a desire that more of this sort of restful Sunday afternoons at home, with all the family together, might characterize our American life. For in genuine domestic enjoyment the English seem to me far ahead of ourselves.

Somewhat of the same impression was received at Lady Henry Somerset's, for one of the clerical members of the party said: —

The Book of the Pilgrimage

The elegant yet homelike rooms, and the little chapel in which service is daily conducted by herself will ever bring to my memory what is most beautiful in home surroundings, truest in home devotion, and highest in personal consecration.

One of the youngest male pilgrims expressed a similar sentiment in this graceful tribute to her ladyship: —

The great things in life are not all in outward experiences; many of them are in inward impressions which prove vastly more inspiring. Our visit to Reigate was of this class. There is no need to eulogize upon the exceptional advantages of lineage, position, and wealth which place the things of this world within the grasp of Lady Henry. It is a great thing for a woman so situated to live above worldly things. It is a greater to dare the abuse, contumely, and misrepresentation in which her choice of a life work will inevitably involve her. It is greatest to do these things with a sweet, strong courage. Those of us who spent a few happy hours in that beautiful, historic mansion will remember less of the house than of the gracious and magnetic personality of our hostess. We recognize in consecration, courage, and faith the great things of life. There is no inspiration so potent as that of a lofty character.

The occasions which contributed directly to the quickening of our Christian faith were frequently mentioned, especially the hallowed service in that little cellar of Bradford's house at Austerfield. An Englishman who accompanied us to Holland was struck with the Christian Endeavor meeting held in the dining-room of the hotel in Leiden, led by one of the youngest of the American laymen, and said of it:

It was a unique gathering of all ages from all parts of America and England, but all inspired by the same spirit. Speeches from men and women, laymen and ministers, short and to the point, no waiting — a verse, a hymn, a sentence — truly we are one family, one people, one nation. My week's journeying with our cousins from over the sea has helped me to understand them better and has made me love them with all my heart.

The same person voiced the general sentiment in saying: —

My chief interest was not in the places we visited, but in the people who composed the party and their doings. There was a peculiar friendliness, a common bond of loving sympathy, which seemed to permeate every individual as though all interests were one. There was not a jarring note, for all were inspired by the thought, "By love serve one another." As an English stranger, I was charmed by the frank heartiness with which I was received and the evident desire to make me feel quite at home with every one.

Another place which appealed deeply to the religious nature was Stonehenge, whither some of the party went from Salisbury, and is thus described by a ministerial pilgrim: —

Standing amid those circles of great gray stones, some fallen, some toppling, a few erect, the silent witness of a bygone faith, the England of to-day — its cities, its navies, its colleges, its cathedrals — seemed to vanish. So likewise appeared and vanished the England of Alfred, of the Roman and the Briton, bowing at the feet of Wodin and Thor. A dim, shadowy land appeared wherein man and his works were as nothing, and nature, wild and savage, oppressed and terrified his spirit. But groping after a knowledge of the unseen Power which he felt lay

Looking Backward

behind the forces of nature, he set up his altar and raised these pillars of his rude and mighty temple. So, for a moment, I was with the silent throng who once worshiped there and felt with them the awful problems of life unenlightened by the Sun of Righteousness.

The influence of the scenes at Bedford and Elstow are feelingly portrayed by another clerical brother in these words: —

Somehow while there, looking upon the village green, or listening to the words of Dr. Brown, or going into the quaint little cottage, or standing before the beautiful statue, or all combined, I was lifted into a kind of ecstasy. I saw John Bunyan as I had never seen him before and felt the strange spell of enchantment which will, I trust, abide until the day of death, making me always and everywhere devoted to the humble and yet immortal work to which every minister of Christ is called.

English views of our Dutch trip are reflected in these clever comments by that prince of traveling companions, Dr. Mackennal: —

One of my earliest and most abiding impressions has been wonder that buildings, public and private, whose age is indubitable, should have so little of the aspect and charm of antiquity. The reason lies in the incorrigible cleanliness of the Dutch people. The dust of centuries cannot gather where the mop is being constantly used. Mystery dwells with cobwebs and the fretting mouse. The buildings too are kept in so ostentatiously good repair. Sentiment lingers where men take pleasure in the old stones of Zion and favor the dust thereof.

His emotions on visiting the scenes connected with Pilgrim and Puritan history are graphically set forth in this testimony: —

In Brownists' Alley, an unsavory lane opening on a dirty little court, we were shown a house which quite possibly was the meeting place of the church which came from London in 1593, and the home of many of its members. It is a tenement house, with closely packed, ill-favored rooms, now occupied by ill-fed, hard-featured, uncleanly men and women. I was strongly impressed that so my spiritual ancestors, many of them, must have looked while they were in Amsterdam. They came here from Naardam, a tidy, self-contained, self-sufficient little town, whose people were kind to the strangers but had no need of them. I felt the humiliation, as well as the suffering, which drove the broken-hearted church back to England again. Under the next reign what did Independency become?

Professional interests naturally colored certain experiences. For instance, our "beloved physician" greatly prized the opportunity of visiting the hospitals in Plymouth, Lincoln, and London, while a minister recorded as among his most agreeable recollections his preaching for the first time in an English Congregational church, and his enjoyment of the charming and delicate hospitality of the elegant home in which he was entertained.

Although, as has been said, our chief enjoyment came from meeting people, yet impressions from scenery and other impersonal sources were by no means lacking. One lady expressed herself as

fortunate in having had my first glimpse of England by way of Plymouth, where I saw not only historic England, but a beautiful England under the early morning sun and vivid coloring of sea

The Book of the Pilgrimage

and sky, and the picture was far beyond my expectation. Another, a gentleman, said: The drive out from Plymouth upon the Devonshire moors, by the gracious invitation of Mayor Bond, on a perfect June day, with the charm of English landscape, seen after a week on shipboard, made up an afternoon not soon to fade from memory.

Others noted the skylark, Shelley's own, "that singing still dost soar and soaring ever singest," the shimmer of poppies among the growing grain, the ivy-colored, picturesque ruins, and the sunset shadows cast by century-old trees on the ancient moat at Wells. The phenomenally fine weather, with only two partially rainy days in six weeks, and the profusion of flowers everywhere in evidence, were also spoken of. The flowers were never lavishly, but as it were lovingly, displayed, and their refining presence gladdened every meal, whether served in lowly inn or lordly hall. At every hotel, even in wayside places like Bawtry where we tarried for only a forenoon luncheon, mine host never failed to add this aesthetic touch to his table. In some places, notably at Farnham Castle, where Mrs. Davidson, wife of the bishop, herself arranged the flowers, and at the Priory, Reigate, the floral decorations were delicately artistic, the scheme of color being in perfect harmony with all the surroundings. Whether it were a single rose in a slender crystal vase or a mass of blossoms in a jar of costly faïence the taste in each case was exquisite.

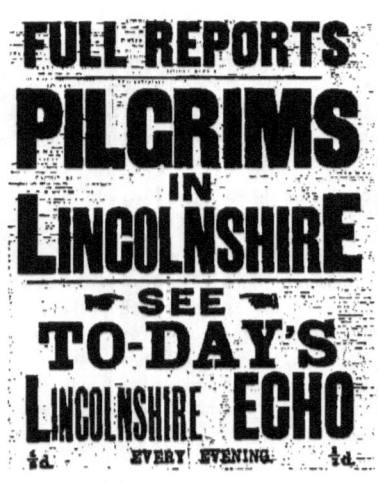

Facsimile of Poster; size of original, 19 x 24 inches.

One pilgrim, not afraid to express his gratification at creature-comforts, emphasizes the joy he experienced in making the intimate acquaintance of the English strawberry, most glorious of all fruits of the earth. We found it at Plymouth when we landed and said good-by to it at Norwich, where it ministered to our pleasure in worthy company of the thick yellow cream from Mr. Colman's dairy. Three weeks of English strawberries, selected for us by hospitable English hosts from choicest English gardens and heaped upon our plates with characteristic English liberality! No wonder that at least one pilgrim for the moment forgot his enthusiasm for Old-World Shrines in his satisfaction with Old-World Strawberries.

At first we were puzzled to understand how the people everywhere seemed to know of our advent, for Britain's "tight little island" is invaded by thousands of Americans every summer without attracting the least attention. When we bought the newspapers, however, the mystery was explained. We found that the local press was devoting from one column to an entire page to our movements and the history around which they centered, and as these were usually chronicled a day or two before our arrival, no wonder that the hearts of the people were in expectation. These accounts were often quite scholarly, and the work, as a whole, far superior to what would be found in the ordinary provincial journal here at home when reporting such an event. The printed poster and the bulletin were frequently pressed into the service of The Pilgrimage, as the facsimile of *The Lincolnshire Echo's* bulletin on the opposite page witnesses. The Lincolnshire papers, particularly the *Yorkshire Daily Post*, a Conservative organ and therefore less likely to be in sympathy with representatives of democracy, showed a most cordial spirit. Several of the illustrated papers, as the *Sketch* and the *Queen*, gave large space to scenes of Pilgrim interest. The leading London papers, too, like the *Times, Chronicle*, and *Pall Mall Gazette*, gave generous recognition, often editorially, of The Pilgrimage. Even *Punch* waxed eloquent over us in this kindly quatrain: —

> Good luck to the new Pilgrim's Progress!
> Hate is a monster, strife an ogress.
> The Mayflower's gone, but with good will,
> Our mutual love *may flower* still.

The only discordant note from the press came from the *Church Times*, the oracle of a section of the High Church party, but the venom of its ill-natured utterances was turned into sweetness by the living words of brotherly love from the lips of some of the highest ecclesiastics within the Establishment.

In closing it may be pertinent to ask what advantages accrue from a journey of this character? Wherein does it differ from the ordinary trip to Europe undertaken by multitudes of our countrymen every season? Most of all in the enrichment it must inevitably bring to one's Christian life and in the deepening of denominational loyalty. He must be a lukewarm Congregationalist indeed, who, after visiting these sacred shrines, remains indifferent to a denomination which has such a peerless history. Patriotism, too, is kindled by a fresh study of the Puritan movement, out of which, to a large extent, emerged our own glorious nation. Other advantages are summed up by a Boston merchant, who had made tours in Europe and Asia, but who acknowledged this to be the superlative pleasure of his life in respect to travel.

In a measure (he says) the blessed benefits we have experienced will be distributed to those who remained at home, for these weeks will serve to give to life a new charm, to home new attractions, and to society new themes of conversation, as well as new sources of instruction and profit. More than all else will come the enlargement of our own natures from contact with our fellow-men in other lands, especially the land which only seven generations ago our ancestors left for New England's shore. We learn better to know that we are all akin, and that the human family is God's household in which we are only a part, with no more or better claims upon his universal goodness than the rest.

Whatever shadows may lie athwart the future pathway of the New-World Pilgrims to Old-World Shrines, the yesterdays of the summer of 1896 will ever "look backwards with a smile." For the space of a few brief weeks we realized, in the words of "rare Ben Jonson," that "in short measures life may perfect be."

The Book of the Pilgrimage

A Word about the Closing Days.

The chronicles of *The Congregationalist's* Pilgrimage, written by Miss Frances J. Dyer of our editorial staff, with a rare sensitiveness to impressions of historical associations, architectural grandeur and beauty, social life and natural scenery, have been mainly confined to England, since there the pilgrims received attentions which make that part of their journey most memorable. The letter, giving an account of the stay in Holland, well illustrates our experiences on the Continent. The week in Amsterdam, with excursions through the country districts on the canals, the Sunday in Cologne with the cathedral service and the Christian Endeavor meeting at our hotel, the day on the Rhine, the visit to picturesque old Heidelberg, the journey through the Black Forest, and the festal splendors of Baden Baden linger in our memories as a succession of wonderful dreams.

At last we found ourselves at the excellent hotel on the Rigi Kulm, with snowy Alps piled one above the other in majestic masses resting against the evening sky, while around the Lakes of Lucerne and Zug, far beneath our feet, electric lights shone like reflections of the stars. After dinner we gathered in the Red Room to spend our last evening as a party together. There a number of pleasant things happened of themselves. Dr. William E. Park proposed thanks, which were voted unanimously, to Messrs. Henry Gaze & Sons, for the admirable provision made for our comfort as travelers through the whole of our journey. Through their excellent business arrangements special trains and carriages on railways, comfortable suites of rooms at hotels, with meals at hours most suited to our convenience, had been placed at our disposal. They had not only made good their promises, but had exceeded them in thoughtful foresight, making it easy for us to do what we came to do with the least possible fatigue and expenditure of time. Next, a hearty tribute was paid to our conductor, Mr. F. E. Murrell, the agent of Messrs. H. Gaze & Sons. Beyond question he had won the friendship of every member of the party, not only by his quiet and assiduous attention to their wants, but by his experience of travel, the culture and the courtesy which made him always a welcome companion. Mr. Murrell is an ideal conductor for a pilgrimage in Europe. Nor was the enthusiasm in the least lessened when a pretty gift was presented to the fair young Greek wife, to whom English, French, and German languages were as familiar as her own, and who accompanied him on this journey that they might spend their honeymoon together.

At this point it seemed as though the meeting ought to be brought to a close, but Rev. W. W. Leete claimed the privilege of expressing his gratitude to *The Congregationalist* for arranging so valuable and delightful a pilgrimage; and this he did so felicitously that every one else was moved to emulate him. The person who had presided up to that time found himself in the background, and this paper would turn rosy red if the kind words of appreciation there uttered were to be printed here. At a late hour Dr. Robie led us in a tender prayer of thanksgiving for the care of our heavenly Father which had so lovingly manifested itself in all our journey, and

A Word about the Closing Days

after making arrangements for a reunion next year the company gradually vanished with strains of gay music ringing in their ears. Next morning we were let down the steep mountain-side to the tender mercies of the blue Lake of the Four Cantons, on whose bosom we were borne to Lucerne. A few hours later some of us were speeding toward Paris, others to the musical festival at Bayreuth, others to Italy, North Germany, and Scandinavia, while half of our number still clung together, and, with Mr. Murrell, turned toward the Alps and buried themselves in the heart of the snowy hills. Some are still wandering beyond the sea. But the New-World Pilgrims to Old-World Shrines remain one company in spirit, and will revive their experiences together in coming days.

Boston, September 1.

A. E. Dunning

BEFORE LEAVING ENGLAND Dr. Dunning sent the following letter to the English press. It was published widely both in London and provincial papers: —

Dear Sirs, — *The Congregationalist's* American pilgrims on leaving England desire to acknowledge through the press their sincere gratitude for the continued courtesies they have received from the time of their landing at Plymouth, on the eleventh of June, to the day of their departure, on the second of July. The Congregational churches, the committee and coöperating friends, have wisely planned and publicly extended to them warm welcome at every place they have visited. Free Church councils have through their committees offered formal and carefully prepared, but not less cordial, greetings. Receptions have been given to the pilgrims by mayors and leading citizens in several towns and cities. Bishops, deans, canons, and other clergy have afforded them every facility for inspecting the cathedrals and churches they have visited, and have besides extended to them hospitalities which have been greatly enjoyed. Masters and professors in the Universities of Oxford and Cambridge have freely given their services to make the visits of the pilgrims to these ancient seats of learning most profitable and enjoyable. The English newspapers, editorially and in news columns, have given generous space to our pilgrimage, and have treated its purpose with great intelligence and discrimination. They have honored the Pilgrim Fathers who settled in New England and have duly recognized the principles of religious liberty for which they stood and which have been incorporated into the United States of America. The British public, so far as it has recognized our presence (and it has done so wherever we paused on our journey), has shown a cordial interest in us as Americans and a warm esteem and friendship for our nation.

We take this opportunity of expressing our gratitude to the many whom we could not personally address, for the kind attentions which have deepened our love for our mother country and our esteem for its people. Our sense of kinship for them has been strengthened and our wishes made more earnest for the prosperity of Great Britain in all that is worthy of her history and her greatness. We leave these shores reluctantly, and bear with us memories long to be cherished of the homes of the Pilgrim Fathers and of the homes of many esteemed friends in England.

A. E. DUNNING,
Editor of The Congregationalist.

NORWICH, July 2, 1896.

Pilgrimage Perspectives

I.

SO the charge of the twoscore and six Congregationalists is completed! Then they came back, but not — not the forty-six. We went out *en masse*. We returned by installments. In early June the Pilgrim persuasion in this land of "stars and stripes" delegated us to traverse the main, and *Gaze* upon the land of our ancestry, ecclesiastical and lineal.

"We came unto the land whither thou sentest us." There is no minority report. The land is fair and fat. If wood is wanting, brick is abundant. There are cities both walled and diked. "The people be strong that dwell in the land," and if they have Anaks in ability, so have we, just as big and as brave. The land is goodly, flowing with tea and tarts. The fruits of centuries of Christian civilization we found in abundance, and each has brought back a heavy cluster to share with friends.

We cannot say with Caleb, "Let us go up at once and possess the land," for, forsooth, we are already possessed by it. We plead guilty to an unconditional un-Miles Standish surrender. England and America are one and inseparable in the divine destiny; their language is common; they think the same high thoughts and cherish the same noble aspirations. Christianity controls both continents. Cables connect under the vast deep; and on its bosom the swift ships, like shuttles, are weaving the web of commerce which both nations are to wear. Both should have the same morals, the same manners, and the same money. England in her heart has no hate for her offspring; and America cannot discard her heredity, for she cannot "run away from her backbone."

English Congregationalists of course most heartily received us into their haunts and homes, their churches and pulpits. Reluctantly, but royally, the parting guests were speeded. But how about the enemy ecclesiastical, the persecutors of our Pilgrim parents? History did not repeat itself. The Anglican Church has repented, and it is not yet the eleventh hour. True, the "old leaven" may not be wholly "purged out," but even our patron saint, Calvin, had to admit that the Christian, though supplied with "special grace" and with a will "wholly inclined toward holiness," still possessed "remnants of indwelling sin." Certainly the Episcopalians treated us after the apostolic injunction, for when we were hungry they fed us, and when we thirsted they gave us drink, and glowing embers, which accrued upon our heads, were fanned into an undying flame of admiration and affection by unsparing effort and kindly attention.

Pilgrimage Perspectives

We have nearly lost sight of our text. Perspectives depend upon position. Vistas vary according to the viewer. Accounts through the secular press have given hints of pilgrimage happenings. The interesting and instructive weekly letters of "F. J. D." leave little to be added as regards places and persons, experiences and lessons. The composite impression has been developed. The delicacy of touch and beauty of shading will be missed in these pilgrimage perspectives, for here the point of view is masculine and ministerial, but the contrast may be suggestive. If these observations seem a trifle tardy, remember that Bancroft asserted that history can only be fairly and fully written until fifty years after it happened.

Every hour since our return the vision of the visit has grown more glorious. The rose tinge in the memory has changed from "mermet" to "jacqueminot." The only criticism we can construct is the total lack of discomfort, disagreeableness, and disappointment sufficient to serve as contrasts.

The chief charm was the company. We were a goodly people, even if we are conscious of it. Christian came before Congregational. We realized our responsibilities as representatives. "Blood will tell," and we tried "to do credit to our bringing up." True to the traditions of our polity, the party was not solely male or female, young or old, clerical or lay. The majesty of membership in a Congregational church was maintained. Equality of personal privilege was preserved. Suffrage was not limited to size or sex. Individualism was cherished, while fellowship was emphasized. The merchant and minister met in "elbow touch." The physician and pedagogue secured a symmetry of body and mind. All the ladies were "elect," whether married or maiden. How unsatisfactory and un-Congregational if the party had been all men or all ministers. Could we have spared the two members with the sweet, unconscious graces of girlhood, the enthusiasm of youth, and the charm of perfect manners? Verily not.

We were a company of plain persons, without gaudy apparel, glitter of gold and flash of gems, but whenever we faced bishops, met a mayor, confronted a canon, or strayed into the haunts of royalty, we turned with commendable pride to the two fine types of young Christian American girlhood and said within ourselves, "There are our jewels." What a "goodly fellowship of the saints" has been realized! A week on a steamer is worth a year's residence in the same neighborhood, and a month of travel more than a lifetime receiving and returning calls. Which one of us can ever sing in sincerity the hymn, "I'm a pilgrim and I'm a stranger"? The latter rôle is obsolete. Even England ruled out this hymn, for as soon as our feet touched the shores of Devon we were all "changed in the twinkling of an eye" from strangers to brethren beloved.

There is a freemasonry of Christian hearts which forestalls features and names, defies distance and transcends nationality. Still the palm comes not without toil, and if you are a pilgrim you must bear the penalty. You must preach, and you must eat. You must act and appear so as not to disappoint those who place you on the lofty pedestal of imagination. The "prophet is not without honor" proverb is still in force. Once we were noted, and found a people who appreciated us. We rose to the occasion. Our spokesman, equipped by travel, the pulpit and editor's chair, "did us proud," and, like the immortal poet of the nation we visited, did not repeat himself. The one who carried the name, and the blood, and the office of the famous Leiden pastor inherited no sinecure. Perhaps he may be pardoned if in the heat and burden of the day he lapsed into pious profanity, and exclaimed, "Shade of my ancestor!"

Politically, the Pilgrimage Party was representative of the New World. Not all of the talk was of theology or travel. Protection had its advocates. Independents of necessity were there. Silver had its supporter — not a ranting, long-whiskered, tangle-haired type, but an intelligent, informed, quiet, lovable, conscientious Christian Congregationalist, and the pilgrims "were not able to ignore the wisdom and the spirit by which he spake," but he did not suffer stoning. Prohibitionists paid a visit to the Lady Somerset shrine.

"What shall I more say? for time would fail me." The plates in the pilgrim kodak are used. The pictures are in the solution of memory. There are no negatives, all is positive. The pictures will be printed indelibly on both mind and heart.

Themodfoule.

II.

Responding to the editorial request for some note on THE CONGREGATIONALIST'S PILGRIMAGE, I, as one "behind the scenes" of it, ought first to testify to the intense eagerness shown by all classes of English people to welcome the visitors, and the happy impression they individually made upon their hosts and hostesses and all who came into contact with them. Persons of all social stations and diverse official positions evidently regarded it a high honor to entertain or in any way contribute to the enjoyment of the visitors, and much disappointment was caused by the numerous invitations which had to be reluctantly declined. Probably the members of the party did not fully realize how they thrilled any assembly in which they appeared. It was the thought of the history that lay behind them, of what they represented, that laid hold of the imagination of the English people and secured ready entrance into their hearts, homes, and places not easy of access. Only an Englishman, or one long resident in this conservative little country, can properly estimate the value of the privileges which the pilgrims enjoyed. Some English Congregationalists could not refrain from remarking that their American brethren had received courtesies never offered to them. One happy incidental effect of The Pilgrimage was to bring together in amicable association many members of the two great divisions

Pilgrimage Perspectives

of the Church of Christ in Britain — Anglicans and Nonconformists — who had not before met, or to strengthen relations already existing. The pilgrims constituted a sort of hyphen or bridge which united, at least for the time being, some who had hitherto kept aloof from one another. The Pilgrimage also served to recall to both Anglicans and Nonconformists history apt to be more or less forgotten. "Churchmen" were reminded of the great principles for which Independents stand, and Congregationalists were inspired with fresh zeal by having their glorious traditions brought so vividly before them. Interest in The Pilgrimage has by no means died out on this side. Applications from people anxious to read a consecutive narrative of the tour continue to be received, and allusions that still appear from time to time in the English press show that The Pilgrimage has made a deep and abiding impression upon the "fourth estate," which, of course, is the most thoughtful and important section of the community (!). Whilst reputable Americans are always welcome visitors in this country, and whilst any members of the recent Pilgrimage who return to these shores will be received with added cordiality, it is generally felt that the Pilgrimage as a Pilgrimage cannot be repeated. The idea was an altogether happy inspiration; it was carried out in a worthy manner and at a most opportune time; but some things can only be done once, and *The Congregationalist's* Pilgrimage of 1896 will rank in history as unique an event as the sailing of the Mayflower.

The probability that one of several happy results of The Pilgrimage will be the establishment of closer relations between American and British Congregationalists is regarded with great satisfaction by members of the denomination on this side. Dr. Dunning's suggestion that the National Council and the Congregational Union of England and Wales should discuss topics of mutual interest and exchange delegates will not be lost sight of at the Memorial Hall. It has several times been remarked that The Pilgrimage has strengthened friendly feeling between England and America, but no one can estimate how great and far-reaching has been its influence in this respect. The visitors came at a critical time, and there is not a shadow of doubt that their intercourse with influential English men and women, and the large space devoted by the newspapers to recalling the ancestry of the pilgrims, recording their movements, and reporting the peace-promoting speeches delivered along the route by representatives of both countries, did much at this juncture to shape public opinion in the right way on the eastern and possibly on the western side of the Atlantic. Should a quarrel between England and America ever again seem imminent, the memory of fraternal hand-shakes and sweet intercourse, of eating together at one table, and of fellowship in worship will surely go a long way in averting such a catastrophe.

Albert Dawson

The Book of the Pilgrimage

June 21. '96

Dear Sir

I regret exceedingly
that it is out of my power
to be present at the On
ten sagions for the Reception of
the American Congregational
Pilgrims, and I must
take this opportunity of
pressing my husband
to speak for the brethren beloved
of these hearts there who

Intended for teachers and
political liberty in this
land and then went to
establish freedom beyond
the sea.

With every reverence
to Inverkeithing

Believe me
Yours faithfully
John Watson

Autograph Letter from "Ian Maclaren."

Henry Gaze & Sons, Ltd.

ALL transportation and hotel arrangements for *The Congregationalist's* Pilgrimage were intrusted to the tourist agents, Henry Gaze & Sons, Ltd. Their efficient management was an important factor in the success of the enterprise, and a word regarding this well-known firm will be of interest.

The business was established in Southampton by Henry Gaze in 1844, and later was transferred to London. Under Mr. Gaze's brilliant management it was rapidly enlarged until it covered all quarters of the globe and embraced every department of travel. Henry Gaze was a remarkable business man: bold originality, great executive ability, strict integrity in dealings both with patrons and employees, combined with intellectual ability, insured success, and these qualities he impressed upon those who were associated with him, and to whom the business was eventually intrusted.

Beginning with modest excursions from London to Paris, the firm extended its operations, until now it has its own system of travel tickets available by all leading railroad, steamship, and diligence transportation lines throughout Europe, America, and the Orient, and covering about sixteen thousand miles within the empire of India. It has also perfected a comprehensive hotel coupon system.

H. Gaze & Sons, Ltd., has branches in the principal cities of the Old World, around the world, and in the United States, the head office for the latter and for Canada being at 113 Broadway, New York. R. H. Crunden, LL.D., is the American manager. To him and to the New England agent, Mr. W. H. Eaves (201 Washington Street, Boston, Mass.), the pilgrims are indebted for unusual courtesies. The booking of the party was in their hands, and Dr. Crunden, in conjunction with the London office, arranged all preliminary details pertaining to *The Congregationalist's* plan of travel.

Alfred H. Gaze, Esc.

In the fifty-two years of its existence the firm has handled hundreds of thousands of tourists, both in personally conducted parties, and also with independent travel tickets, according the fullest facilities at reasonable rates.

The present corporation is managed by five directors: Mr. Alfred H. Gaze, managing director; Mr. Harry E. Gaze, his brother, who has charge of the shipping department in Europe; Mr. W. Edwin Gaze, the president of the Thewfikich-Nile Steamship Company, and manager of the Paris and Oriental branches; Colonel E. Bance, and Dr. R. H. Crunden, who is general manager for the United States and Canada.

R. H. Crunden, LL.D.

The St. Denis Hotel

NEW YORK seems especially dear to the pilgrims as it does to every American traveler who has watched its high buildings fade away in the distance when the ship puts out to sea, or has eagerly scanned the horizon for the first glimpse of them on the return. Of the many pleasant scenes perhaps no one will be more pleasantly remembered by those of the party who were quartered at the St. Denis Hotel, than the graceful spire and beautiful grounds of Grace Church which add so much to the attractive environs of this comfortable hostelry.

It has been the cause of no little comment that the St. Denis has remained in its present locality at the corner of Eleventh Street and Broadway, while so many of its contemporaries have moved farther up town, and at the same time should have increased its large patronage. The reason for this is, no doubt, its admirable management at the hands of the proprietor, Mr. William Taylor. While most of the other hotels have changed owners, Mr. Taylor has remained in charge of the St. Denis, and given to its administration his personal attention. The excellence of its cuisine, the always attractive and homelike appearance of the house, and its air of quiet refinement, are witnesses to the value of his careful and constant supervision. The St. Denis is a favorite resort for professional and literary people, the large publishing houses being within easy walking distance, and the appointments and surroundings of the hotel itself peculiarly congenial to them.

The St. Denis occupies an ideal location, being in the heart of the shopping district and of easy access to all points of interest and amusement, as well as to the piers of the transatlantic steamship lines. It is situated midway between the upper and lower, or social and commercial sections of the city. This hotel was chosen by the proprietors of *The Congregationalist* as the headquarters for the parties of both The Pilgrimage and The Oriental Tour, a reception to the latter company being given in its spacious parlors the day previous to sailing.

Taylor's Restaurant, which is connected with the hotel, has acquired a national reputation, the table and service being unsurpassed. In order to meet their increasing patronage and also accommodate private, college, and society dinners, an extension has been made on the Broadway side which includes a new café and banquet halls. These are all connected with the main part of the hotel, and together with it are equipped with all the modern conveniences.

The Hamburg=American Line

THE pleasant voyage across the Atlantic on the fleet steamship Columbia, of the Hamburg-American Line, was by no means the least enjoyable part of *The Congregationalist's* Pilgrimage. The magnificence in the appointment of the ship, both as to its accommodation and service, made the six days on the ocean full of rest and comfort.

The fleet of four steamers, consisting of the Columbia, Augusta-Victoria, Fürst Bismarck, and Normannia, which is used in the weekly express service of this company between New York and England, France and Germany, is unexcelled in point of convenience, safety, comfort, and speed. The first two named are sister ships, as are also the last two, and all are models of marine architecture and the equals of any vessels afloat.

In conjunction with the North German Lloyd Steamship Company, the Hamburg-American Line conducts a German-Mediterranean Service. Magnificent steamers make regular trips to Algiers, Naples, and Genoa by way of the Straits of Gibraltar. This route is exceptionally attractive to travelers bound for Europe who wish to avoid the rigors of the North Atlantic in winter; also for those Orient bound, this being the most direct line. *The Congregationalist's* Oriental Tour of 1894 took passage on the Normannia, which was at that time running in this Mediterranean Service. During the months of January and February the Hamburg-American Line despatches one or two express steamers from New York to Alexandria, touching at the Azores, Gibraltar, Algiers, and Genoa, thus accommodating the large and constantly increasing winter travel to Egypt and Palestine, and offering unusual facilities for reaching these countries by the shortest route.

The Twin Screw Mail Service, consisting of steamships Persia, Prussia, Patria, Phoenicia, Palatia, and Pennsylvania, runs to Hamburg direct. These ships are about the same size as the other express steamers, and are equally well equipped for the promotion of safety and comfort. The Pennsylvania is even larger, being the largest carrier afloat. The steadiness, even in the heaviest sea, of the ships used in this service has been highly praised by passengers who have crossed on them.

For several years the Hamburg-American Line has organized during the winter season excursions to the Mediterranean and Orient, placing at the disposal of travelers one of its floating palaces. These cruises have become so popular that they have now inaugurated a summer tour to and along the coast of Norway, the first of which was made by the Columbia this year. These cruises afford all the comforts and luxuries of life.

The aim of this transatlantic line has always been to give the best service possible. How near they have reached the acme of comfort, speed, and safety is well attested by their magnificent fleet and the popularity of their ocean service at all seasons of the year.

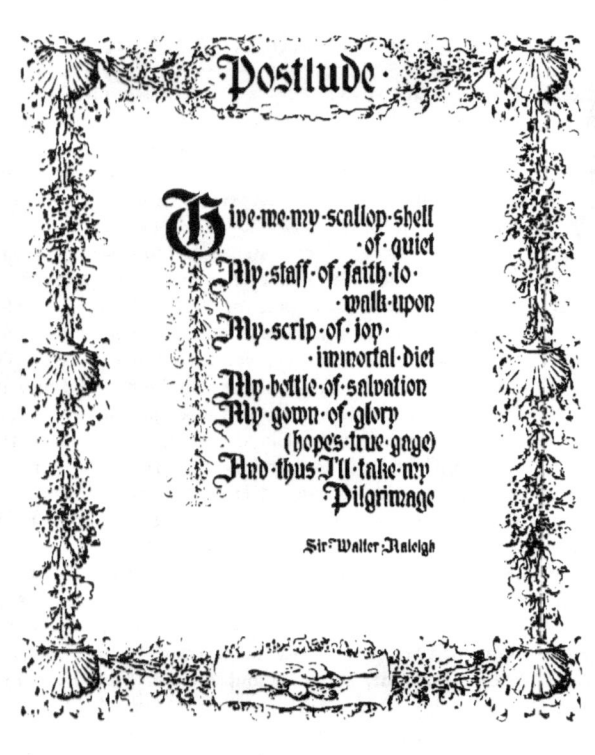

Postlude

Give me my scallop-shell
       of quiet
My staff of faith to
       walk upon
My scrip of joy
       immortal diet
My bottle of salvation
My gown of glory
       (hope's true gage)
And thus I'll take my
       Pilgrimage

Sir Walter Raleigh

Autographs

J. Townsend Maxwell   T. I. Kightley

J. T. Bond   G. W. Bath: & Well:
J. A. Bond.

W. Austin Evans.   Walter P. Hogben

Walter J. Edmonds
Canon of Exeter Cathedral   Edward Massan

Chas. J. Atherton   George David Boyle M.A.
Treasurer Henry Rickenham Dean of Salisbury
of Exeter Cathedral.

                J. H. Bourne
Norman H. Smith.
                Edward F. Pye-Smith.

G. L. Dickinson.   Alex. T. Mackennal

Arthur Rayner Dyer
Mayor of Winchester

Wm. T. Woods

Andrew Mearns

Randall Wiston:
Edith M. Davidson

J. Guinness Rogers

W. R. Wood Stephens.

Charles A. Berry
Robert Horton

A. M. Fairbairn   Newman Hall

Joseph Parker
Wm. Mottram

F. B. Meyer
Christ Church

G. G. Bradley
Dean of Westminster

W. T. Stephenson

William Sinclair

Yours faithfully
Frederic W. Farrar

Isabel Somerset

P. T. Forsyth

Jane E. Stewart

H. Montagu Butler

Halley Stewart

S. Munsey

Albert Dawson

E. Munsey

Sincerely Yours
John Brown

David Barnett

Jno Thomson

William T. Rudershaw

Thomas Hornblower Gill

J Clarke
Mayor

John Stephenson

Yours very faithfully
J D Jones   William Armagh

Edward Hurison

The Palace Norwich
John Norwic.

J. Clements. M.A. Sub-Dean
& Canon Residentiary of
Lincoln.

Most truly yours
William Ripon DD

Hugh S. Griffiths.   J. Coleman.

Charles W. Stubbs

George S. Barrett   Faithfully yours
                     William Barrett

Maud Jeffries

John Lewes   14th of September 1896.

www.ingramcontent.com/pod-product-compliance
Lightning Source LLC
Chambersburg PA
CBHW020303170426
43202CB00008B/480